WICCA 101
Compendium

BY KEN HOOKER

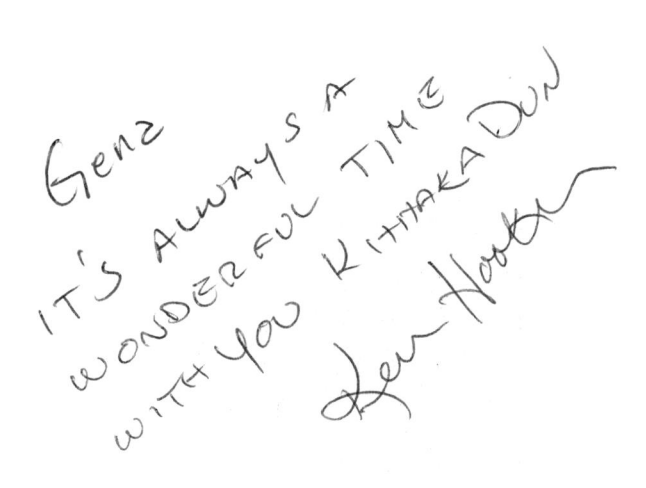

*Gena
It's always a
wonderful time
with you Kittakadun
Ken Hooker*

DORRANCE
PUBLISHING CO
EST. 1920
PITTSBURGH, PENNSYLVANIA 15238

The contents of this work, including, but not limited to, the accuracy of events, people, and places depicted; opinions expressed; permission to use previously published materials included; and any advice given or actions advocated are solely the responsibility of the author, who assumes all liability for said work and indemnifies the publisher against any claims stemming from publication of the work.

All Rights Reserved
Copyright © 2022 by Ken Hooker

No part of this book may be reproduced or transmitted, downloaded, distributed, reverse engineered, or stored in or introduced into any information storage and retrieval system, in any form or by any means, including photocopying and recording, whether electronic or mechanical, now known or hereinafter invented without permission in writing from the publisher.

Dorrance Publishing Co
585 Alpha Drive
Suite 103
Pittsburgh, PA 15238
Visit our website at *www.dorrancebookstore.com*

ISBN: 979-8-8872-9427-8
eISBN: 979-8-8872-9927-3

WICCA 101
Compendium

Ken Hooker

BIFROST

These are my memories, from my perspective, and I have tried to represent events as faithfully as possible.

Cover art by Raquel Hooker

AUTHOR BIOGRAPHY

Ken Hooker was born in 1961 in Cape Girardeau, Missouri. Growing up in the California Bay Area, he was fascinated with sword and sorcery type stories that lead him to learn martial arts, fencing, and archery in a drive to be like the heroes of the early swashbuckling films. Later, he developed a love of Scuba diving that has taken him all over the world to see the underwater world as maybe Captain Nemo once did. As a young adult, he studied seminary as a Christian Missionary but ended up joining an eclectic Unitarian Church that had a more open approach to deity.

Some years after that, Ken gained his ordination with the church. This training led to more exposure to the craft. When open rituals piqued his curiosity about the Wicca, he joined a wicca 101 course and then got initiated one year later as a 1st degree Gardnerian. He spent many years studying different traditions such as Gnostic, Mythraic, Faery, and Alexandrian. Once he achieved his 3rd degree, he hived off and formed a coven with his wife, Zoe (who is also a 3rd degree Gardnerian HPs). They have held several Wicca 101 courses since moving to the South and he still enjoys being the High Priest of their learning coven to this day. *Wicca 101 Compendium* is his first book.

Acknowledgements

I want to take the time to thank all the people who taught me Wicca as I grew up, all the way from a 'baby pagan' to the 'grown up' HP I am today. Also, I would like to thank all my students as well, who helped mold the Wicca 101 courses I did as a Gardnerian 2nd and 3rd degree High Priest. To my publishers who patiently molded the words you see into something more legible than the mishmash of broken thoughts from one moment to the next. My wife and HPs who actually supported my wildly crazy scheme to place our class into something others could enjoy or hopefully work through to get a better grasp on the Craft or Wicca as a whole.

With all the books, webpages selling initiation, Wicca 101 online courses, or the stuff you get on Pinterest, it is a wonder that so many people are unaware of the red flags some of this self-aggrandizement generates amongst the more traditional Pagan people of today. So, with that said, I would also like to acknowledge you the reader who is possibly stepping out on a limb to learn more or taking that first step in learning about yourself and the calling of the Craft that is in your heart. If you are a more advanced student of Wicca and are thinking of holding your own W101 course, I hope this assists you in setting up the course and syllabus for yours and thanks for trusting me to help in that.

Table of Contents

Introduction 1
What is the Craft, Wicca or Paganism 13
Ethics 23
Deities 37
Mythology 47
Different Traditions 59
Sabbats 69
Grounding and Meditation 77
Divination 85
Chakras 101
Tools of the Trade 139
Energy and Magic 155
Sacred Space 171
Dedication and Initiation 185
Recommended Reading 201

Chapter One
Introduction to Wicca

This compendium provides a solid foundation to Wicca without limiting the reader to one tradition or path. Embracing both the spiritual and the practical, Wicca 101 Compendium is a primer on the philosophies, culture, and beliefs behind the religion. Since so many books out there now speak towards focusing on their path or provide a jumble of information with no cohesive formatting, we offer a tried-and-true format based on the syllabus of our Wicca 101 course we have taught for many years. As a 3rd degree Gardnerian High Priest for over 30 years, I have developed a comprehensive course that can share the basics we use to teach aspiring Witches and assist in leading them on their path, whether that be as an initiate or a solitaire or something in between.

Some people believe that the Wicca is just another fancy term for the Craft or Paganism and will use them interchangeably. I disagree with that way of thinking, and we will dive into that in chapter two on how I view it all. Suffice it to say that while Paganism can be an 'umbrella' for multiple types of religions, it is more than Wicca, and in today's ever-expanding world, of neo paganism, BTW (British Traditional Wicca) etc., there are many different faces to the religion. Since Paganism in itself does not have a standard doctrine, per se, like some of our main religions do, it makes this a more open, and welcoming religion that embraces our world and nature.

In today's world of urban technology, immediate gratification via social media, the ever-changing society of divisive politics, I see more and more people turning to the quiet, calm, self-actualization, associated with Paganism. The massive number of seekers who wish to learn outweigh the amount of teachers available, so they turn to books, webpages, social media, etc. to try and learn about Wicca, but some of what you read is outdated, factually inaccurate or driven to a specific tradition. This book will be based on my practical experience from teaching the Wicca over many years, so I do not reference back to other authors' books. (Except in my recommended reading list) The desire for us all to reconnect with nature, the divine and your own inner spirituality is a driving force in today's youth just as much as it is with some of the older amongst us.

Perhaps other people in your circle of acquaintances will think your studies odd and be afraid. There are many hundreds of years of mistrust on Pagans, the Craft, and the 'power' of a witch. Some indeed did harm and wished ill on others, I am sure, just as many 'Christian' men did the same in the name of their religion... neither is excusable, but the use of your religion as a scapegoat diminishes you, your faith in the divine, and those you try to beguile.

However, the same can be said that many performed healing and helpful workings before science took over from herbalism, civilization from simple living and gave credit to the powers above (or the Earth). Sadly, that distrust of the Wicca is reborn in today's world with some folk and their fear of the unknown that makes them scoff at things they don't understand. I feel we have a responsibility to the Wicca that you try to help others understand, but also that it be done in a tactful manner as nothing is more annoying than a proselytizer! Once you actually achieve some learning and skills, be it through self-dedication or initiation to a coven, you are in a position of knowing while the others around you may be on the opposite end of the spectrum.

It is incumbent upon us as Wiccans to show we are helpful or perhaps as the Cunning Craft-folk of old, to keep this to yourselves to preserve the Craft. If help is needed, it will be sought, so you need not advertise your powers, knowledge, or ability to commune with Nature and the God or Goddess. A wise man once said, *"With great power comes great responsibility"* (Thanks Uncle Ben from the Spiderman comics) and in so many ways that is true. In our classes we strive to teach that the Wicca provides a tool in the Craft that can have great things accomplished, but the use of that power has some responsibilities that we will discuss later.

Due to the sheer number of Wicca 101 books on the market, many newcomers to Wicca find themselves piecing together their Wiccan education by reading a chapter from one book, a few pages from another, or burrowing into each and every book they can find and think they are now a witch. While I would never say that someone is not a witch, if that is the way they lean, to me, they are a witch. What we offer that is different from many of the other options is that we review vital techniques and philosophies that may or may not be taught by others or with the exercises and meditations, circle scripts, we walk you through them step by step so you can easily understand the importance.

This does seem to lead to a very eclectic and convoluted learning path that may or may not cover some very basic things we have learned are important to your ability to grow as a witch. One of the things we note in our classes is that when you read book "A" it will say this is bad, while book "B" will say that that is a good thing to do. So, yes, sometimes the information can be confusing. That is why I think 'book smart' is not always the best avenue to pursue, but to push for some real practical experience. I should also say, however, to me, there is a difference between book smart and actual practice.

There is definitely a difference between working solo and in a group/coven environment. A friend once said that working solo can be done in a porta potty as it is all in your head and does not require any space, tools, or other foci. While working in a group or coven setting means interaction with multiple people, like in an orchestrated band to produce a beautiful piece of art. While his analogy is quite apt, although a little crude, it makes a point that simply shows a dramatic difference in styles that can also be used to show a difference between book smart and practical smart. Book smart is all in your head, but the practical smart is real world experience. Many teachers will tell you to work slowly and cautiously, so as not to overextend, or put yourself in danger.

We will tell you to work at your own pace and trust you to know when to speed up or slow down as this is a self-paced experience, and we all grow or learn at different speeds. To be clear, however, do not read this book in a week and think, "See now I am a witch as I read this book!" You must practice, practice, and then practice some more to insure you have the skills and experience to push energy, create sacred space and protect yourself and any others you may end up working with.

I know in a book it may not be as important to make note of, but in a classroom environment or even when you do gain access to a ritual or public gathering, etiquette is a primary thing to be aware of for almost every person in the ritual or gathering. Most of the people will be from a myriad of cultures, races, genders, sexual leaning, etc. There will be a smelting pot of all these different persons, religious backgrounds and of course, temperaments and energy movement skills. Use good manners, don't grab, or touch other persons items without being given permission. Hugging is seen as a generally accepted thing at many open gatherings, but some people are not 'touchy' or just don't hug, so always ask before doing so. If a circle is delineated by some markings prior to the start, such as candles, painted/drawn on the ground, or even with small rocks, please be cognizant of this and try not to pass over the lines even prior to the creation of sacred space. I say this, as with most magic, the ritual starts with the intent, so by the leaders already starting to lay this out, they are already setting up that space and passing over it may affect the creation or stability for later on.

At some point, most people will have an athame, cords, alters, chalices, or many other items for assisting in the creation of sacred space and while we will speak on these separately in chapter eleven, it is important to know that at some point you may want to get these items. These should be personal to you, simple reflections of your beliefs and if you are in a public area, like in a dorm room, simple enough to not draw attention if you are trying to stay private. If you do not already have one, I would start my search for an athame which 'should be' a black handled, steel blade, double-edged, knife you can carry easily and while it does not have to be sharp, I would recommend that it be sheathed for easy carrying. Many old guard Wiccans feel you should make it, but most of us do not have access to the tools or other requirements for forging a blade so I feel in today's age, you can purchase one and then just ensure you cleanse, purify, and consecrate the item prior to use. Again, we will speak more on that in chapter eleven.

At the foundation of Wiccan belief is the premise that everything in the universe, both real and spiritual, is inherently interconnected. This means everything has an energy field, can be effected by magic, or used as a tool or foci in a spiritual aspect…kind of like, for all you Star Wars fans out there. . . The Force. The farther you progress in the Wicca the more you realize that your spiritual health is interconnected with other parts of your physical health, which is connected to the outer influences of the area you live in, your neighbors, the groups you work with, your friends, pets, everything. Just as you, in turn, influence everything about you in a reciprocal symbiotic relationship.

Wiccans, in general, can be both pantheistic and animistic. (The belief in many Gods and the belief that all things have a soul) With many Wiccans believing in reincarnation, a cycle of life, death, and rebirth which is emphasized by the wiccan calendar. When you look at it from a big picture aspect, it starts at the beginning of the year with life being created…the planting of crops, the seeds germinating. Spring comes and things bloom and grow, then fall arrives with its harvests to be gathered to survive the winter months of darkness, when we start all over again in the next year. It mirrors our lives in that we are born, grow up into adulthood and then reap the harvest of hard work.

As we continue to grow older, we become enfeebled and must survive our older years in some level of less comfort until we pass. If you believe in reincarnation, it just starts again later!

As a religion, Wicca offers what all religions offer: a philosophy of life, a sense of where we belong in the cosmos, an understanding of our relationship with the plant and animal kingdoms of our planet and home, and a form of worship through which we can participate in the mysteries of the life force and fulfill our needs for shared human activity by doing this with others. It offers self-actualization, based on learning, positive interaction with others and growth spiritually through many different acts. What it does not offer, is a form of control through guilt, or a hierarchical based system of authority throughout the pagan world as each coven group is autonomous in and of itself. (Yes there is some hierarchy of HPs/HP to coven members, but not this coven is better or of a higher authority than that one) So, while you may not click with this group here, you may be a perfect fit to the group over there!

While Wiccans find the sacred in all of the universe, most localize immediate reverence in nature, the earth, the moon, and the sun. They gather in circles when celebrating and worshiping in order to honor the cycle of life they perceive both in nature and in their own lives. Their holy days are taken to be rites of passage, marking the emblems of each cycle, solar and lunar events known respectively as "sabbats" and "esbats". Sabbats being the eight yearly seasonal celebrations, (Which we speak on later) while the Esbats equate to the Full Moon cycle

Belief in free will and in the ability to affect this systemic universe leads to the belief in magic, generally defined by many in the Wiccan community as: "The art of creating change in accordance with your will." As a mystery religion, Wiccan practices maximize opportunity for the personal experience of the mysteries. The deep personal journey of self-realization and conscious evolution performed by a Wiccan initiate is one of the highest forms of magical intention. Think of it as a self-improvement course!

Janet and Stewart Farrar sum it up well: "To the witch, self-development and the full realization of one's unique potential are a moral duty." To put it succinctly then, it is your job as a Wiccan to continually improve yourself and to grow as a witch. Initiation into increasingly deeper mysteries is done in stages, otherwise known as the degree system (frequently three-tiered). Vivianne Crowley, Wiccan priestess and psychologist, gets to the heart of the matter:

"The Pagan mystery religions were systems through which their initiates came to understand the true nature of reality and also their own inner nature: who and what we really are. Often, we share an old saying with the classes: "Through exposure to teaching, ritual and symbol, the doors of perception were opened; the windows of the soul were cleansed; and unto the initiate were revealed the mysteries of the Gods and of their own inner psyche: all they were and all they had the potential to be."

This kind of delineates what Wiccans can use to self-improve, to cleanse your spirit so it can be closer to the divine and act as a guideline to what you must practice. As I stated earlier, there is no centrally accepted theology or dogma in Wicca as you might find in Christianity, Islam, Buddhism, etc. Accordingly, individual Wiccans are encouraged to develop their own relationship with the divine. Most incorporate both polytheism and monotheism, drawing upon the myths and spirituality of multiple cultures. The divine is also seen by many as a multifaceted One (called by some the Goddess); others choose to interact with countless male and female facets of the divine One.

Within Wicca many "paths" are recognized, including Traditional Wicca (e. g. , Gardnerian, Alexandrian, Hereditary), feminist Witchcraft (e. g. , Reclaiming, Dianic), eclectic Wicca, and solo practitioners known as "solitaries". All these possibilities to me are like Lutherans speaking to Protestants. Both see their path as the right one, and to each it may be. It just does not make the others a bad or wrong choice. You could (and frequently I do just to open the minds of our Outer Court) give this example, but make it about being between Muslims and Christians, so it drives home how we are affected by our beliefs.

This leads to great discussions on the church as a whole sometimes which I think is a good thing. We ask that you think not through the dogma of the church, but through the opened eyes of a bystander and you may see my point that both offer the same, peace to all, but approach it from a different angle. Who am I to say which is the more correct…for you, me, or anybody? Someone wiser than I once said something about casting the first stone in a glass house…

The Wiccan community consists of covens, traditions, and solitaries. The autonomous coven is the basic group structure found in the Wiccan community. These covens serve many purposes, serving as a center of group worship, clergy training, and sometimes as a "family" of choice. Covens are small (rarely over ten people), intimate groups operating in full autonomy, and therefore without accountability to any external "authority" like a denomination, a given tradition will define and support a set of ritual practices that its member covens hold in common.

When covens exist within the larger community (i. e. , of a tradition), they will usually follow similar training schedules, with similar rites and rituals. Traditions often convey lineage, a common ancestry, which is sometimes accompanied by greater respect and acceptance of authenticity within a community. Relationships between tradition members frequently mirror actual family relations. It must still be remembered that despite the similarity of covens within a given tradition, covens and coven leaders will generally be considered autonomous.

Solitaries are those Wiccans *not* working with a coven. Some do receive their initial training in a coven, while others are entirely self-trained. Twenty to thirty years ago, the solitary path was not always accepted as a legitimate path to the Wiccan mysteries. The enormous growth in seekers referred to above has challenged and now even altered this norm. As the tremendous influx of seekers desiring training outstripped the existing resources of covens and teachers, many turned to Wiccan literature and relied on their own personal experience for their training. This is seen quite literally in so many open rituals or even on multiple internet boards where more than a two to one ratio of seekers vs teachers exists. The amount of seekers outstripping the teachers has, in my mind, forced a paradigm shift in that you now hear of 'self-dedication' being as accepted as an initiation and I would agree with that under certain circumstances. For generic Wicca or Paganism, it would be acceptable, but I would not classify myself as a self-taught Alexandrian and think that that should be accepted by the greater whole.

Now may actually be a good time to discuss the differences

between a 'Red' or 'Green' coven so you can be aware of potential issues you may want to steer away from. Generally speaking, a 'Green' coven will not ask for money to learn, will not charge for services, initiations, or for coven needs. They will also not involve sex as currency, or as a 'part of the learning process' or require pictures of you skyclad. While working skyclad is common in many initiatory traditions, most people do not see it as naked as you will be wearing your magical accoutrements. Gerald Gardner, the Farrar's, Valiente and many others espouse it as allowing you to be 'closer to the divine' but do not hold it as a voyeuristic thrill. Part of the charge of the Goddess even says: "and you shall be naked within my rights." This is (certainly in my mind and teachings) done as clothes create hierarchy, and that is not what we want to espouse in the worship of Lord and Lady.

On the flip side, a 'Red' coven is one that does practice sex as part of the Craft, may charge for services or learning, etc. This should be a red flag (no pun intended) as to the veracity or intentions of the group. While I have seen some groups like this, the general community as a whole recognizes this as a group to avoid and generally will steer you away from said group types. It is always best to check with the local Esoteric or Occult book shops as they may have info on the group you are attempting to work with. Of course, you can also check social media for the areas various groups to see what the reputation is like. Social media has a lot of misinformation but can be a useful tool for searching out the reviews of said group.

Also, just to be clear, while I may be clearly making a 'shade' comment about the internet, I do so, so that you do not believe everything you read on the internet…except that I am a French male model! <Wink> If the group, you are attempting to work with say they are Gardnerian or Alexandrian, as an example, you should be able to view their lineage to back up who they say they are. Anyone who refuses to show you this, may be hiding something in the worst case, or they just may not have it as tightly and cleanly prepared as it should be in the least case, but it should be a red flag that some things may not be completely kosher.

I recall a time we went to New Orleans with my family and the children were just beginning their journey with Wicca. I was searching for a specific dye (Wode) and one lady in her shop got somewhat testy about never having heard of it and when questioned about it, I mentioned we used it in the initiation process. When I told her we were a Gardnerian Fam. Trad. She exploded and demanded I remove myself from her store naming me a pervert, 'sicko' and all sorts of derogatory pejoratives. It was not until we were home that we learned of a gentleman who was posing as a Gardnerian and acting as a red coven leader to entice younger girls into a sex cult. The whole reason for that story is to show, that these groups are out there, so please be careful!

Chapter Two
What it is and what it is not

With all that's been said, let's start with the definitions of Wicca, Craft and Paganism so we are all on the same page as to what we are speaking on. I took these straight from Wikipedia, so you can easily review, but this will be how I describe each.

> **Wicca** is defined as: A form of modern paganism, especially a tradition founded in England in the mid-20th Century and claiming origins in pre-Christian religions.
>
> **The Craft** is defined as being short for Witchcraft which is a form of sorcery or the magical manipulation of nature for self-aggrandizement or that of a client.
>
> **Paganism** is defined as a religion other than the main world religion, specifically a non-Christian one.

I realize some will use these terms interchangeably, but I use Wicca as the religious group name that tends to be initiatory, while paganism (or even today's Neo-Paganism) is the overall umbrella name and generally is not considered initiatory in my mind. The Craft, magic, ritual, spell work (whichever name you prefer) is the tool used for change.

For me, this means that Wicca and Paganism are a religion, or the worship of Deity/Nature/Divine. That deity may be some grouping from your favorite pantheon, a pairing of a God or Goddess, a singular all-knowing entity like Yahweh, the Dryghton, or even the divine in yourself or the Earth Spirit. What or who or how you worship is all up to you, and I would be remiss if I told you otherwise. The other interesting part of this for me is that the Craft is then just a tool used in that religion. Like any other tool, it is not inherently good or bad, but its results can be molded much like a surgeon's scalpel.

If the surgeon uses it to remove an ugly painful kidney stone from your left kidney, it has done its job in a manner that you are happy with the good results. However, if that same scalpel is used to remove the wrong kidney (in this case your right one) that tool was used improperly, and you would be unhappy with the results but would blame the surgeon and not the scalpel. That is how I view the magic of workings in our religion. The magic spell being cast or crafted is not inherently bad or good, but the **Intentions** of the caster are what is to be judged. To continue with the analogy above, if I create a spell to relieve you of kidney stones and you feel better, you are a happy camper, but when you lose that kidney due to my imperfect use of the craft, you should be upset at my sloppy use of the craft and not the magic itself.

The point here is that it is not the craft itself that is good or bad, but the way it is used. This tends to remove the 'black' vs. 'white' magic that so many people get caught up on. It is not the magic (scalpel) that is good or bad, but my use of the tool. I bring this up as so many people, including those who want to label Wicca as a bad thing, try to use the 'types of magic' as justification for their closed minds. I often also use this as a quick segue to speak on the Three-fold law for a moment. With your casting of magic, you should also keep in mind the three-fold law. If you are not familiar with the term or phrase, it tends to be used to mean that any actions you do, will return to you at three times the output you expended.

So as an example, it is NOT if you gave someone a dollar, you may receive at least three dollars back at some near point. Think of it more as if you do one dollars' worth of Good or Bad, then in the near future you will receive the same as compensation. The same can then be said for your charms to do good, vs. your charms to create harm. This is part of our ethics conversation later as well, and I know some people absolutely hate that discussion, but it is a valuable one for many people.

While many people read books on the different types of Wicca out there, be it Gardnerian, Alexandrian, Fairy, Dianic or esoteric Wicca, these books are written towards those traditions aspects. The path we will take is a more generic one that covers items like meditations, grounding, the pantheons, chakras, tools and simple ceremony or ritual as if you were going through a yearlong wicca 101 course taught by us many times with the end goal of giving an individual the needed basic knowledge to help you make an informed decision on if this is the right path for you. Later in the book, we will speak on ceremony, ritual and even the Wiccan calendar so you can understand some of the basic ways to celebrate the occasion.

You may have already read about how in the early years of Wicca, it was a secret religion as the practitioners kept to themselves to avoid ostracization or direct persecution. Some history of Wicca may still be needed as it is often spoke about from a secular or even wrongly interpreted through historic documents that may have been deemed accurate at the time. Although there were precursors to the movement, the origins of modern Wicca can be traced to a retired British civil servant, Gerald Brousseau Gardner (1884–1964). Gardner spent a great deal of time in Asia, where he became familiar with a variety of occult beliefs and magical practices. He also read widely in Western esoteric literature, including the writings of the British occultist Aleister Crowley.

Returning to England shortly before the outbreak of World War II, Gardner became involved in the British occult community and founded a new movement based on a reverence of nature, the practice of magic, and the worship of a female deity (the Goddess) and numerous associated deities (such as the Horned God). He also borrowed liberally from Western witchcraft traditions. Following the repeal of England's archaic Witchcraft Laws, Gardner published 'Witchcraft Today' in 1954, founded his first coven, and, with input from its members, especially from Doreen Valiente, developed modern witchcraft into what we today know as Wicca. It spread quickly to the United States in the late 1960s, when an emphasis on nature, unconventional lifestyles, and a search for spirituality divorced from traditional religions were especially in vogue. It is almost comical that his potentially strained relationship with a few, created the name for his tradition which we now today call Gardnerian Wicca. (This was meant as a pejorative)

Covens, which ideally number 3 to 13 members and are typically entered through an initiation ritual, sometime align with one of many distinct traditions. As coven members master the practice of magic and become familiar with the rituals, they may pass through degrees of initiation. It is often said that the First Degree is for learning the craft, the Second Degree is to start teaching it. The third degree is for those who wish to enter the priesthood. In Gardner's system, priority is given to the priestess, with leaders in the Gardnerian community tracing their authority through a lineage of priestesses back to Gardner's coven.

Despite variation within the Wiccan community, most believers share a general set of beliefs and practices. They believe in the Goddess, respect nature, and hold both polytheistic (belief in many Gods) and pantheistic (all things are part of the divine) views. Most Wiccans accept the Wiccan Rede, which is an ethical code that states: "If it harm none, do what you will." Wiccans participate in rituals throughout the year, celebrating the new and full moon, (the esbats) as well as the equinoxes, solstices, (the Sabbaths) with the four main celebrations of Imbolc, Beltane, Llughnasadh, and Samhain.

Many Wiccans may call themselves witches, a term which many individuals today still identify with Satanism. As a result, Wiccans are continually denying any connection with Satan or devil worship. It is important to note here that Satanism is still a belief in the Christian religion, albeit a corrupted version that puts the devil on high as the symbol of control. To put it succinctly, Satanism either believes in an atheistic approach or a theistic one that puts the power with the Christian Devil who is in battle against a controlling God. Since Wiccans tend to steer away from the Christian orthodoxy, it is inherent that their belief in Satan (or service to him) would even be considered as something that worked as a matched set. Wiccans on the other hand, believe again, in a polytheistic view where many Gods or Goddesses have power, or in a Pantheistic view where all things are part of the divine. The other most common misconception is the use of the upside-down Pentagram vs the Pentacle. The upside-down Pentagram is typically used as a representation for the head of Bahamut or the Devil. The Pentacle, or star inside a circle, is often thought of as the four elements of earth, air, fire, and water ruled over by spirit and held together in a sacred circle.

This confusion also assumes that Wiccans believe in this religion as 'the one true religion' whereas a Wiccan will speak on many religions having merit but still tend away from Christianity as but one path to follow. Because of this stigma created by the church itself, in an attempt to subvert the people to follow Christian ways, way back in the early years of the religion, it created a separation of Wicca from the Church that still exists today. History has shown however, that many higher up leaders of the Christian church at that time may have practiced some of the witchy ways by using herbology or sympathetic magic to help cure ailments. I am sure that many realize today that the church at that time 'commandeered' the many 'pagan' holidays by giving them new Christian names so people could say they were being good Christians.

Again, I would remind you that Wicca is thought of as an initiatory religion that is a subset of Paganism, which is all other religions that are not part of the larger accepted church style religions like Christianity, Islam, Catholicism, etc. Wiccans have also attempted to establish ties with other polytheistic (Germanic or Celtic) and nature-oriented (Native American) religious communities in an effort to distance themselves from the thought that Wicca meant Satanism.

By the 1980s there were thousands of Wiccans in Europe and North America. Although the growth rate may have slowed by the end of the decade, Wicca has once more gained increasing social acceptance and has even diversified to include numerous variations on the original teachings and rituals from the 50s and 60s. As Wicca and Paganism moved into their second generation, belief faded in the notion that Gardner had inherited a set of witchcraft rituals and practices that had been passed on through a tradition with unbroken ties to pre-Christian paganism.

Although many Wiccans once cited the work of Margaret Murray, in support of their belief in the ancient origins of their religion, they now generally recognize that Wicca (as we know it today) began with Gardner and his associates. Today, Wiccans are found throughout the English-speaking world and across northern and western Europe. Although once an esoteric book shop was a thing of rarity, today they are plentiful. This speaks to how this tradition is now an accepted venue. A great example is when you visit New Orleans and journey through the French Quarter area of town, you will find a plethora of new age/occult/esoterica shops as well as some excellent museums i. e. the Marie LaVeau shop/museum that offers tours for a nominal price.

In our Wicca 101 course, we often speak about how this is an exceptional change not only for the better, but also as a barometer on how the world is changing and possibly heading back to a reverence of nature, despite, or in retaliation of, the environmental impacts we see in America due to politics, social media, and the rampant dependance on technology.

As alluded to earlier, most Wiccans use a duo-theistic approach with the God and Goddess. Some groups will have specific names that are public, while others may have 'secret' names taught only to initiates. This brings up a great opportunity to speak about how this is a male and female vision of the world and cosmic order but note also that both the God and Goddess can be multi-faced. Such is the case with the Maiden, Mother, Crone, the three faces of the Morrigan (Badb, Macha, Nemain) or the Triform aspect of the Goddess Hecate (Dark, Waxing and Waning). These many faces of the Goddess represent different stages of life, attitudes, strengths, weaknesses, even some vastly different energies when worshiped. It is noted that the number '3' is important in magic just like so many other numbers, such as 4, 5, 7 and 9.

The number two speaks about the duality, polarity, the God, or the Ying and Yang. The number four is used to represent the four elements, the four quarters. The number five is mentioned as being the four elements, plus Spirit which you may recall mentioning just a short while ago while talking about the Pentagram. The number 7 is due to its association to the lunar cycle or 28 days (or 4 x 7 which brings it all around. Lastly is the number 9 which is basically, 3x3 to make it triply important! This numerical importance carries on even to the different aspects of the God: with the Sun and Holly King, or the lord of Death and Rebirth to show that duality or the importance of the number two. In the tradition my coven currently operates, we say that these dualities are faces seen by the individual, or aspects needed at specific times to assist in a working.

Since there is male and female in all things, we tend not to get caught up in the LGBTQ squabbles, but state that the High Priestess rules the coven, and the High Priest is the strong arm of the law. This makes for a malleable change when practicing the light and dark times of the year where it switches on who casts and runs the circle, according to some traditions, but it also proves the truth that there is male and female energy in all of us. While I may not be a 'good hard Gard' and hold to traditionalist conservative views, I believe that if Gerald was right that there is Male and Female, good and bad, God and Goddess energy in us all, then it stands to reason, in my mind, that a trans person would be accepted as the sex they present to the world and not the sex between their legs. This should not prevent them from operating in the religion or even in how they interact with the God or Goddess. Again, just my opinion!

Now just a few quick words on etiquette. Beyond what you learned as a kid on why you put each utensil at each location when setting the table, keep your elbows off the table, don't slurp your drink or soup, etc. There is also some commonly thought of forms of etiquette you should be aware of while with other Pagans.

For instance, never touch another person's ritual gear without asking. This is kind of a big one as some may have spent hours cleansing, consecrating, energizing, etc. a special piece and may be very picky about any other energies it is exposed to. Yes, I would question why that special piece was brought to a public environ anyways, but a small amount of personal respect goes a long way. I also tell our students that while today many people are more open about their religious leanings; it is still good manners to not walk up with a stranger and introduce them to your HP and HPS as such: "Hey, let me introduce you to John and Jane, my HP and HPs. This is Tom my friend from work!"

This creates not only an awkward position for the High Priest and Priestess to respond in a positive manner but does not consider on whether they wished to remain anonymous or that someone nearby may have heard and is a raging hard core anti-pagan that just got told the names of two individuals who are now noted as not being 'of the right religion' in their eyes. Many Pagans tend to be more open and allow hugs and displays of affection, but some do not, so naturally, please don't just assume the people you are meeting for the first time are 'huggers' or that you can touch them in any manner beyond accepted social norms.

In a circle (assume public as it would be explained in detail at a private ritual) realize that again, not all are at the same level, so critiquing another participants skill, energy levels or grammar may not be bad etiquette so much as bad form. While you may think it is OK to correct someone, or even be happy when it is done to you in public, it shows a lack of empathy. Pull them aside later and explain what they did and how to fix it next time in your opinion. This gets us back to that golden rule thing of treating others as you wish to be treated and I believe most of us are a little embarrassed to be called out in public.

Many others are not aware, but when walking into an area that is already set up, please be cognizant that it may have already been consecrated, outlined or already have the intent to work pushed into it, so your walking in and out, over the delineated lines, or blowing out of candles, may upset the balance the leaders are trying to set. Some groups perform ritual purification with baths, scourging, censing and asperging prior to the invitation to enter sacred space, so be aware of your surroundings and listen or feel what your instincts are telling you.

Chapter Three
Ethics

I have noted in my past that this discussion is either completely hated or excitedly engaged in. I hope that my dry approach to this along with some examples for self-discussion at the end may 'pique your interest' as a potential eye-opening experience as opposed to just some lecture you *had* to listen to at school.

Professional counselors and Wiccan clergy are healers in a similar vein who must share similar ethical responsibilities: they have a common duty to prevent unnecessary human suffering and to aid in the healing process when suffering occurs; they serve as guides on the path of self-realization, taking on the roles of teacher, supervisor, evaluator, and counselor: and their positions and/or status may be somewhat duplicated, but in no way do I believe that a Coven leader is a trained therapist. I am a good listener and will gladly do so when approached, but when it comes to offering a technical diagnosis, I do not have that certificate. I can listen but will recommend advice or sometimes simply refer them to a known specialist who can maybe assist in a more clinical venue.

All of this clearly suggests that counseling ethics are relevant discussion and important factor to Wiccan clergy, and that

Wiccans in general would greatly benefit from a study of professional ethics as part of their training. Just as counselors recognize the importance of cultural awareness, regularly assisting individuals and groups in their search for value clarification, it behooves Wiccan clergy to do the same. Ethics is based on well-founded standards of right and wrong that prescribe what humans ought to do, usually in terms of rights, obligations, benefits to society, fairness, or specific virtues.

Ask yourself what ethics means to you, does it mean something relevant to the religion, is it just something you should do, or did you have replies like the following:

> "Ethics has to do with what my feelings tell me is right or wrong."
>
> "Ethics has to do with my religious beliefs."
>
> "Being ethical is doing what the law requires."
>
> "Ethics consists of the standards of behavior our society accepts."
>
> "I don't know what the word means."

These replies might be typical of almost anyone as the meaning of 'ethics' is hard to pin down, and the views many people have about ethics are somewhat shaky to say the least. Sadly, many people tend to equate ethics with their feelings. But being ethical is clearly not a matter of following one's feelings. A person following his or her feelings may recoil from doing what is right. In fact, feelings frequently deviate from what is ethical.

Nor should one identify ethics with religion. Most religions, of course, advocate high ethical standards. Yet if ethics were confined to religion, then ethics would apply only to religious people. But ethics applies as much to the behavior of the atheist as to that of the devout religious person. Religion can set high ethical standards and can provide intense motivations for good ethical behavior. Ethics, however, cannot be confined to only religion nor is it the same as religion.

Being ethical is also not the same as following the law. The law often incorporates ethical standards to which most citizens subscribe. But laws, like feelings, can deviate from what is deemed ethical. Our own pre-Civil War slavery laws and the old apartheid laws of present-day South Africa are grotesquely obvious examples of laws that deviate from what is ethical.

Finally, being ethical is not the same as doing 'whatever society accepts.' In any society, most people accept standards that are, in fact, ethical. But standards of behavior in society can deviate from what is ethical. An entire society can become ethically corrupt. World War II Nazi Germany is a good example of a morally corrupt society.

Moreover, if being ethical were doing "whatever society accepts," then to find out what is ethical, one would have to find out what society accepts. To decide what I should think about abortion, for example, I would have to take a survey of American society and then conform my beliefs to whatever society accepts. But no one ever tries to decide an ethical issue by doing a survey. Further, the lack of social consensus on many issues makes it impossible to equate ethics with whatever society accepts. Some people accept abortion, but many others do not. If being ethical were doing whatever society accepts, one would have to find an agreement on issues which does not, in fact, exist.

What, then, is ethics? Ethics, to me, is two things. First, ethics refers to well-founded standards of right and wrong that prescribe what humans ought to do, usually in terms of rights, obligations, benefits to society, fairness, or specific virtues. Ethics, for example, refers to those standards that impose the reasonable obligations to refrain from rape, stealing, murder, assault, slander, and fraud. Ethical standards also include those that enjoin virtues of honesty, compassion, and loyalty. Ethical standards include standards relating to rights, such as the right to life, the right to freedom from injury, and the right to privacy. Such standards are adequate standards of ethics because they are supported by consistent and well-founded reasons.

Secondly, ethics refers to the study and development of one's ethical standards. As mentioned above, feelings, laws, and social norms can deviate from what is ethical. So, it is necessary to constantly examine one's standards to ensure that they are reasonable and well-founded. Ethics also means, then, the continuous effort of studying our own moral beliefs and our moral conduct, and striving to ensure that we, and the institutions we help to shape, live up to standards that are reasonable and solidly based.

With the interplay between the Wiccan Rede and Threefold Law, Wiccan morality and ethics is a far more complex subject than a casual glance would have you believe. Once the additional ideal of Perfect Love & Perfect Trust comes into play, it is obvious that the complexity of the issue of Wiccan morality and ethics can only increase. "Eight words the Wiccan Rede fulfil. And it harm none, do what ye will."

The Wiccan Rede is an interesting concept and whilst simple at first glance, it is far more complex in practice, especially when you consider that the Rede doesn't mention the concept of unavoidable harm – the ending of an unhealthy relationship for example, which may cause harm to the person involved, but will prevent a greater harm in the long run. A great deal of thought must be put into an action as to whether harm would be caused, whether it can be avoided and, if not, whether the harm caused will negate a greater harm.

In my experience, I have known many people on a variety of spiritual paths, to have taken the Rede to be a law or even shortened it to just be "Harm None"; however, it is clear that such a law would be impossible to follow. The word Rede actually means 'advice' and it is therefore a more sensible approach to look at the Rede as a guideline and an ideal to strive for rather than a hard and fast rule. I like to think of it like the bumpers you have down each side of a bowling alley. The ball may veer off course, but the bumper helps it back on track. (and now you know I can't bowl very well also!) This is why I believe the Rede works as a bumper to keep us from veering too far from our paths.

The Rede is a positive way of thinking, giving freedom of personal morality rather than imposing a set of strict religious rules. Quite often when we are told we aren't allowed something, or are told we can't do something, it makes us want it even more. As the saying goes – 'forbidden fruit tastes sweetest'. Where certain religious laws may seek to suppress and contain those elements of human nature that they find distasteful or undesirable, the Rede gives freedom of personal expression in a healthy way. So long as you are not causing harm to others or to yourself, then your morality and individuality are yours to express.

I have heard it argued that such freedom of personal expression would allow for the breaking of non-religious laws and criminal activity, but I would argue that not only is the Rede intended for operation within the law (as would be common sense I like to think), but that there is no such thing as a victimless crime and that any such activity would constitute harm in any case. Aside from this, I am of the opinion that any person given to breaking a law is going to do so regardless of any religious guidelines or commandments.

The decentralized nature of Wicca and the lack of clear group standards place responsibility firmly in the hands of the individual. Wiccans are given the directive to look within—in the "Charge of the Goddess"—which is the most well-loved and widely accepted liturgy of the Wiccan religion: "And thou who thinkest to seek for me, know thy seeking and yearning shall avail thee not unless thou knowest the mystery: that if that which thou seekest thou findest not within thee, thou wilt never find it without thee"

The Law of Threefold Return

I have noticed a tendency to use the word "Karma" in conjunction with the Threefold Law, but it is often a westernized view of Karma, which is applied. In doing this the idea of Karma is interpreted as some sort of universal power that hands out punishments to those who do bad things and rewards those who do good things. Even I earlier used the analogy of a dollar to explain the Threefold law! The Eastern view of Karma, though, is simply that actions have consequences. By being mindful of them, you can earn "good Karma" and thus earn a better future. However, failing to take into consideration the results of your actions will earn "bad Karma" and lead to some sort of hardship as a result.

If the Rede has been (as often occurs) mistaken for a law and is applied to everything, in conjunction with Threefold Law in its misunderstood form (i. e. "westernized" karma), it would be difficult to see how a person could even get out of bed in the morning for fear of causing harm! In my opinion, Threefold Law is actually closer to Karma as it was intended in the East or to the Biblical maxim "You reap what you sow." It is an easier concept to accept if it is not looked at in terms of whatever you send out comes back to you times three, but instead is considered in terms of how our choices are made. In numerology, the number three is representative of divine trinities and of completion (birth, life, death; beginning, middle, end; past, present, future). This lends itself to the idea of Threefold Law representing a completion of our choices, i.e. course of action decided upon, course of action taken, results of action taken.

Combined with the Rede, it is essentially a method of keeping us mindful of our actions and ensuring that we are fully aware of their potential outcomes and impacts. This applies not only to our spiritual lives (such as when performing a magical working) but also to our daily lives. It reminds us that whatever choices we make, there are repercussions and that we must take responsibility for our own choices and deeds. There is no "big bad" to blame when things go wrong, we are responsible for everything we do, good or bad.

Perfect Love and Perfect Trust

I feel that when it comes to Wiccan morality and ethics, this concept is often greatly neglected. But what really happens if you incorporate into your life the "highest ideal" of Perfect Love and Perfect Trust? Is this the same ethos as spoken by Jesus or Muhammad to "Love another as you love yourself?" It is easiest to apply this concept to our coven mates, and it is reasonable that this should be the case; after all, it is with our coven that we first experience perfect love and trust, in the form of initiation. Their trust that we are the right person for their group and the love everyone bears for each other as friends and as part of the wider Wiccan family. Then there is the trust and love that we ourselves express in putting ourselves in a vulnerable position with them, by undergoing the initiation itself.

We could even apply the concept to our family (however you define that) with whom we share a bond of unconditional love and trust. It is sometimes possible to apply it to friends and lovers, although here, love and trust may not be unconditional. Often, trust must be earned, and love is given but not without a certain amount of fear of betrayal or rejection.

So, the question becomes, should the concept of Perfect Love and Perfect Trust be applied outside of the coven environment? Is it even possible to apply it to those people we don't know closely? Perhaps we leave ourselves open to all kinds of mundane and spiritual problems if we try to define our morality further by including this idea away from the environment where it is most often encountered.

Is it even possible to have any love or trust for people whose motivations we don't actually know, let alone perfect love and trust for them? It becomes a little like the commandment, "love thy neighbor as thyself". It's a nice idea in principle, but does it actually work in practice, or does it become something unachievable, which we still strive for? Perhaps the best step we can take is to be good people and to treat others with respect and in turn, earn respect through our actions.

Although there are indeed many traditions of Wicca, Wiccans have one ethic in common which is the Wiccan rede spoken on earlier. Wicca has no concept of sin per se, but it does have a strong system of ethics — the individual laws may vary slightly from tradition to tradition. These ethics are based in a kinship with all things and beings, we believe that we must weigh our actions in relation to the good of all as far as we are able to, not just to others in our group.

What is the role of morality in Wicca? There is no jealous, vindictive god in Wicca, no judgmental and punishing Father. In Wicca the Mother Goddess is primary: loving, nurturing, generous, wise. And the Gods are protective, playful, and strong without violence. Well, generically speaking of course, as some may have some very human emotional aspects <looks at the Greek pantheon> as an example of how they can be somewhat vindictive in the stories.

No guilt, no shame, no violence, no judgement... Wicca is a religion of life, freedom, celebration, responsibility, and growth. Is there death and consequences at the end? Surely. Oddly enough, this worries people! Some people fret that, if we don't have to beat ourselves before God in order to earn forgiveness, if we don't suffer from guilt, won't we run rampant and not care who we hurt?

There are much better reasons to be conscientious and kind, than trying to avoid guilt! When you use your religion to impose guilt to make people be good, they will present a façade of goodness, but perform as if they are the tethered dog who has escaped its chain and run wild when not thinking they are watched. Don't let guilt of a vengeful God dictate your morality, let your concept of ethics, morality, right and wrong dictate on how to handle others and if honest, you will treat them as you hope to be treated. . . almost like that Biblical maxim we spoke on earlier - "You reap what you sow."

A Guilt-Free Religion?

Guilt and shame have nothing to do with remorse, morality, ethics, or virtuous behavior. Real virtue does not come from self-flagellation, but from the desire and intent to choose right action. To associate guilt and shame with virtue is to confuse the whip with the walking. One can walk even better without being flogged! One can live a truly virtuous life only when the motivation comes from within, not from without.

That's one difference between religion and spirituality. Religion imposes virtue on others, as parents insist that children "play nice." Spirituality leads people to find virtue within themselves, and then aspire to live up to it. Wicca is a spiritual path, not a religion of laws based on guilt. It isn't concerned with moral rules, but with ethics — the guidance that comes from the Divine, right into each person's Heart. Thus, the descriptor of Wicca being a self-actualization religion. That's the real difference.

- Morals are cultural or religious rules, that are imposed upon you. You are expected to live up to them, "Because

we say so!" They are like laws, enforced by peer pressure and authority figures.
- Guilt and shame are learned behaviors/emotions designed to keep people under control. They are the enforcers of cultural morality.
- Ethics come from within and shine out into the world through your actions. They are the innate awareness of right-action and wrong-action.

In a way, the current cultural struggle between morals and ethics is the struggle between Power and Integrity - a core paradigm shift that's part of the worldly transition. Morals give people power-over others. Ethics gives people power-within themselves.

Where Does Wiccan Morality Come From?

There are no morality rules in Wicca. But there are inescapable Spiritual Truths...

- <u>Do as you will</u>; be your authentic, divine self.
- <u>Harm none</u>.
- Whatever you give out, <u>returns to you many times over</u>.
- What you resist, persists.
- Your thoughts and emotions create your reality.
- We are all One.

These fundamentals of Wicca are the source of our morality. They create a respect for all life, and responsibility for our actions to a degree that is rarely found in some of the most prominent religions. Wicca avoids making laws, because laws become distractions from truth, and from ethics.

Not to mention, there are always ways around rules and laws. Instead, we become aware of Divine Law. We find a more binding, effective, and eternal law within ourselves. And so, by avoiding morality, Wiccans often end up more ethical than those who accuse them of lacking morals.

As you can see, I think ethics is an important part of the Wicca. Anyone who accepts that magic works, will have come to understand that being able to change things at will brings a certain responsibility. If you study medicine to become a doctor, you are responsible for the health of your patient, and you would do what you thought was best for them in the long run – even if it meant an unpleasant operation or treatment at the moment. Those who practice Wicca are no different and have a similar responsibility to others. People will come to them, if their training was effective, seeking assistance or encouragement in all sorts of difficult situations. The Wiccan is then tied to that person and should try to suggest a solution which is not only right for the present but for a long time as well.

Trying to patch up a broken marriage may seem the right and moral thing to do at the time but in the long run it may leave the two individuals in a worse situation. To heal a lonely old person may appear to be a kindness, but if they are lonely due to no living family or friends, it may not have been so kind.

Removing cancer from your spouse, if improperly or poorly described as to proper intent, may remove the cancer or it may take the organ with, that the cancer was on, now leaving you with a dead or disabled spouse bringing on an even greater pain. Sometimes it is better to act and sometimes it is better to do nothing. No matter what the problem is, it may be better to do nothing than to act in haste or with poor intent that makes the problem even more painful or harmful.

So, from an ethical and moral standpoint, it is always best to research the situation, gain as much information as you can prior to deciding to use the craft to bend nature to your will, certainly you would not want to act out of spite, anger or blinded emotional sentiments while operating a vehicle, so think of the craft as that automobile you drive each day. Is it just a car for transportation or is it a 3,000-pound sword that you wield as a shield against wickedness and evil in some fantasy novel Sir Knight? Slaying dragons or peasants with impunity or unknowing concern...

Chapter Four
Deity

Throughout the lifetimes of humankind, we have sought for someone or something to worship, to ask for help or to call for guidance. In some places these Gods and Goddesses have had specific personalities and names. In other places, these Gods and Goddesses, have been pictured in fire, air, earth, or water and symbolized by natural phenomena. The ancient peoples of the British Isles did not make statues of their deities. They were horrified by the Romans idea of worshiping a living Caesar. To them the Sun represented the God, and the Moon represented the Goddess, but the actual God and Goddess were beyond imagination.

You may recall I made a statement at the beginning of the book something like – "For me, this means that Wicca and Paganism are a religion, or the worship of Deity/Nature/Divine. That deity may be some grouping from your favorite pantheon, a pairing of a God or Goddess, a singular all-knowing entity like Yahweh, the Dryghton, or even the divine in yourself or the Earth Spirit." This is where our discussions will go in this chapter so you can determine how best it is for you, the reader, to follow your path towards divinity. Even though Wiccans may worship the God and Goddess, it is not uncommon for them to draw divine inspiration from other religious traditions.

Pagans are able to recognize many different levels of God and Goddess hood. This includes identifying with archetypal images in myth as well as in a Gestalt approach. Myth is viewed as the sacred drama of the archetypes, and the individual who properly understands this as myth actually experiences and lives the message of the myth, gaining an insight into the mysteries of Nature and God and Goddess hood.

Pagans are able to recognize the differing levels of divinity. They work in ritual and magic with the part of the human psyche and come closest to human understanding. At the same time, a Pagan believes that it is perfectly possible to keep one's feet firmly planted on the ground, while at the same time striving for the transcendental attainment of the absolute or realization of the spiritual achievement. The Wiccan holds that the knowledge of the God and Goddess is found within one's own being when one lives a state of Perfect Love and Trust or in Harmony with the forces of nature and the multiverse.

Wiccan groups differ in the way they view the God and Goddess forces. Today it is very common for covens that are matriarchal to be emphasizing the worship of the Goddess in the religion. Some groups, such as Dianic covens, omit the role of the God entirely and admit only females into the religion. This is in part a reaction to the overt, heavily patriarchal emphasis that our society's religions have taken. In more archaic times, there was probably more of a balance between the masculine and the feminine aspects of the Wicca or Paganism.

Many traditions take a matriarchal stance because it is important at this time in our heritage to balance out the societies heavy emphasis on the masculine and because the human emotions relate better to objectifying the absolute in its soft, warm, nurturing aspect. This in some ways ignores that the Goddess also has a fiery, angry, vengeful aspect as well! This always reminds me of that movie "Species" when the doctor talks about matching the alien DNA to a woman's so it will be more docile and the main character says, "You did not date much did you!?" Of course, all heck breaks out and we see just how fiery, angry and destructive a female can be!

Delving back into the archaic roots of Wicca, scholars differ over theories pertaining to the God – Goddess relationship. Some believe that the God was predominant at first when hunting and gathering was the earliest mode of sustenance, and that the Goddess came into predominance later with the introduction of agriculture. Others say that the Goddess was originally predominant, stating that the maternal role was the only parental role for thousands of years. This is showcased in some pantheons that state the God came about first, while others state the Goddess came about first. Yet others say early humans were able to recognize the harmonious duality of male and female from the very beginning, and that equality in the God – Goddess relationship is the most archaic form.

This all showcases a duality, a yin and yang of the God and Goddess as you see both existing together even when one is pre-eminent over the other, through the course of time, the other rises to the top, for a period, restoring the balance. I say this as even if you run wild worshiping the entire Germanic Pantheon, and that would be a feat worth talking about I think, you would still have a creator, a lawful enforcer competing with the unruly trickster, while others tried to work for peace as others strove for war, some for the arts, others for weaponry. You see a balance even in this polytheism to balance out the powers in harmony. Even reading the struggles of the Gods, a theme exists a tale of creation with the Ragnarök a final Destruction, Loki creating discord and Thor, or some other, helping to fix the chaos.

So, when we speak of Duality vs Polytheism, you can still see many aspects of the Ying / Yang or duality in each of these. But when you drop to a monotheism as is seen by the worship of Yahweh you see an all-powerful being that is omniscient, invisible, ever-present, vengeful, and benevolent. That same duality exists even in this aspect, so I posit that maybe there was always a divine being, but man may not have been able to understand it as a singular aspect and divided it up into easily digestible parts. (Think about the blind man examining the elephant, he reviewed sections of the animal and came to simple conclusions based on what it was he knew at that time) Could the German pantheon or the Greek, Roman, Egyptian all really be just different names for the same easily digestible parts of that one God? When you look at the Dryghton you see a similarity to Yahweh, Muhammad, and others, but with a different name... It is described by many as the following:

Dryghton (pronounced *dricht-ton*, from Old English), is a concept in Gardnerian Wicca that there is a self-aware energy pervading all things and places. It is omnipotent, omnipresent, and, most importantly, difficult (though not impossible) to access. It is comparable to other Pagan concepts such as Akasha, Spirit, the Web of Life, and the Star Goddess (or for the nerd in all of us...The Force). The Dryghton is *"Male and Female; changeless, eternal"* because it is perceived as the source from which all other Deities manifest. There is a prayer of this that can be found all over the net, so I do not think I am breaking any vows by placing it here for your review.

In the name of Dryghtyn, the Ancient Providence,
Who was from the beginning and is for eternity,
Male and Female, the Original Source of all things.
all-knowing, all-pervading, all-powerful,
changeless, eternal.

In the name of the Lady of the Moon,
and the Lord of Death and Resurrection.
In the name of the Mighty Ones of the Four Quarters,
the Kings of the Elements.

Blessed be this place, and this time,
and they who are now with us.

This sounds pretty familiar, doesn't it? I have a close Christian friend who when I shared this, they spoke up saying, "See! We worship the same! You call it Dryghton, and I call it God…you really are just worshipping one singular all powerful God the way I do, so why do you also use all these other names like Morrigan, Hecate, Pan and Cernunnos?"

This started a very long discussion on the differences in ethics, the way we worship vs the way they do, the many different faces of God, how I believe that many of them are shifters in one aspect or another, that maybe they all are and that explains why so many 'Gods' are duplicated from one pantheon to the other. Again, I reference the similarities between Roman, Germanic, Celtic, etc.: different names for a similar deity.

As I mentioned at the beginning of this story, to me, since Wicca or Paganism is a religion, I think however you connect with the divine, whether it be Germanic, Celtic, Native American, The Dryghton or an ancestor, or the Divine within, what is important is that you are following some form of reverence and respect for that divine. Maybe it is a small alter with a candle and incense, maybe it is a fancy, full alter for holding service, or maybe it is a small space on a bookshelf that you have a few pictures, or something you hold sacred representing that divine. It really does not matter what your alter has on it, unless your chosen tradition calls for specific things, but that your intentions are clear, heartfelt, and followed through.

So, with all that said, it should be obvious that Paganism is not based on doctrine or liturgy dictating a specific version of God or Goddess. As said before, many pagans believe and follow the Rede: 'if it harms none, do what you will'. By following this code, Pagan theology is based primarily on experience, with the aim of Pagan ritual being to contact the divine in the world that surrounds them so they can attain a better version of themselves, or a better life in the future.

We touched very briefly on the many faces or aspects of the God and Goddess, but now it's time to review some of the other aspects such as the duality of the two-faced God, the triple aspect of the Goddess, etc. Above, I may have at one point, mentioned the two-faced god, Janus, the Roman god of beginnings, transitions, or doorways, endings. This shows that there is two sides to everything. (Recall that old saying about 2 sides to every story? This is it) War and Peace, Inside or Outside, Dark and Light...This shows a god who presides over new projects or change. The duality of nature. You may have heard of the Oak and Holy kings, always battling for the Goddess' affections, Our New Year's representation of the old year (dressed in old clothes and often depicted as extremely aged, vs. the new Year which is often depicted as a newborn in diapers.

Whether it be the Oak and Holy king, Cernunnos, Pan, or whatever name, it is often said that the God is a Horned God who is pictured with antlers. (I am sure we are all familiar with the pictures of Cernunnos holding a torque on the side of the Cauldron?) I believe these are all one and the same! Sometimes however he is considered the Lord of the Underworld, but I do not think that makes him 'evil' or to be feared, rather he is a part of that circle of life we come to understand is all a part of nature. Remember that in this aspect, he is a father figure, a protector and sometimes guide in helping us commune with the dead.

Then we come to the triple aspect of the Goddess, the most famous is the Mother, Maiden and Crone, but also think about the sigil of the moon Goddess (a Waxing moon, Full Moon and Waning Moon). The Triple Goddess is one of the most important and iconic Wiccan deities. While Wiccans may worship any number of different deities, the Triple Goddess is almost always front and center as she is the primary representation of Divine feminine power for most Wiccans. Let's touch on that aspect just in case it is not familiar to you.

> **The Maiden** – This is the aspect where she is a young vibrant, beautiful woman just starting out in life. This is a representation of new beginnings, purity, consecration, or purification.
>
> **The Mother** – At this point, the Goddess has entered motherhood and is now the maternal protector and the fertile life bringer. We may speak

to this aspect for guidance, love, or celebrate her aspect when we bless the birth of a new child.

The Crone – This is often the name given to an older and more experienced woman in the Pagan society, or the older and more 'seasoned' version of the Goddess. This is not some weak and frail old woman doddering on a cane, this is a priestess in the height of her power! This may be why she is called upon when we need spiritual wisdom, assistance with divination, prophecy and perhaps a bit of intuition.

There are several goddess figures that share this type of aspect or are considered a triple Goddess combination: The Morrigan is always my favorite example (Babd, Macha and Nemain) as these aspects can represent the three above, or a much darker version if not careful.

Lest we forget, this 'triple aspect' can extend to the God with the 'Father, Son, and Holy Ghost' version we get from Christianity or the Trimurti which consists of Brahma, Vishnu, and Shiva.

This just shows that the duality or treble is not specific to just the God or the Goddess but is something shared. I ask the class at this point, what they think, as we have typically spoken about several mythologies, certainly multiple God, and Goddess' and at some point, we talk about how maybe, the difference between the Germanic Pantheon and the Greek is not so much at all, but maybe, they are really looking at the same aspects, but just given them a name in their own tongue?

Wiccan deities are the heart and soul of our religion. Since we are, by tradition, polytheists, the rituals, and spells we create that involve deities bring us closer to the Divine spirit of the Akashic or the overall universe. Multiple Deities help us conceptualize the Divine spirit in a way that our brains can comprehend. They illuminate a particular aspect or facet of the Divine, allowing us to understand one part of this much-larger puzzle.

Deities may have their own personal traits and characteristics, but ultimately, they are all pointing toward the same Divine essence that permeates everything in the universe. As an extended example when Wiccans want to honor both the masculine and feminine aspects of the Divine, you will sometimes hear them referred to as a pair—the Lord and Lady. This approach emphasizes the dual nature of Divinity and how these two Wiccan deities make up a larger whole.

Chapter Five
Mythology

Since we just got through speaking on divinity and some of the myriad possibilities, I thought I would take a moment to share some of the items we normally hand out at our Wicca 101 Classes so people coming into this fresh or blind to all the different pantheons, can see who some of the names are we speak on.

Many of today's Judeo-Christian religions, believe that the universe and everything in it was created by a supreme being. On the flip side, there are plenty of people who will only accept the scientific explanation of the big bang theory. That debate leads one to wonder: "Where do Pagans think the universe, the world, and everything came from? Are there any Pagan creation stories out there?" (The answer to that question is yes, when you look at the different mythologies, but in today's modern world of tech and scientific methods, I think we can accept them for what they are. Potentially just a myth or humans poorer understanding of the world at that time.)

While I doubt you will ever find any concrete information about what Pagans (the people) think on the beginning of the world, it may exist even though I have not found it…because, as mentioned in chapter 2, Paganism is an umbrella term that defines a lot of different belief systems. Because "Paganism" means lots of different belief systems, you're going to encounter lots of different mythologies about creation, the beginning of the universe, and the origins of mankind as a species. Just look at the way it is spoken about in the Bible, Norse Mythology, Greek, Japanese, Native American and you can see vastly different modalities for this to occur.

In other words, there are a vast array of beliefs, in the Pagan community, about the origins of everything, and those will be different from one person to the next, based upon their own individual belief systems. Believe it or not, many Pagans don't assign any sort of great cosmic metaphysical meaning to the origins of the universe at all. While many people *do* follow pantheons that have creation stories, often these are accepted as the way that our ancestors, and early cultures, explained scientific events, but not as hard fact in today's society.

It's not uncommon to find Pagans who accept scientific principles such as evolution as a core principle but also have room in their practice for their tradition's creation stories. As conflicting as this may sound to some, I think it is possible for both of these to be true. Something had to start it all off. Was it Big bang or was it Audhumbla the Cow giving suck to a Frost Giant and creating the world of man, we may never know for sure! But we DO know that evolution is happening as shown by that great ecologist Darwin, so I think both can exist together.

In traditional myths. . . the void often plays a role as the site of original creation. This is its first and most dominant role. In each creation story, order somehow emerges from this sheer absence. The essence of these myths is this ungraspable moment of emergence. And the myths represent this moment in many different ways. While I may consciously and completely accept, on a scientific basis, that evolutionary theory exists, I also accept that within my pantheon, the creation legend detailed in Germanic prose is a legitimate explanation of how things began, but *purely* in a spiritual perspective. In that manner of thinking, I don't have trouble reconciling the two ways of thinking, because my spiritual path is a way that my ancestors understood how things in some Pagan traditions, particularly those that are goddess-based, came into being.

There is a legend that the Goddess created all things herself by giving birth to a race of spirits that filled the world and became mankind and all the animals, plants, and other living beings. In others, the Goddess and the God came together, fell in love, and the Goddess' womb produced humanity. In Native American traditions, there are a number of different creation myths, and they are as varied as the tribes who have passed these legends along through the centuries. In Native American Indian mythology, they believe the great spirit created the world and then with help from the many Animal spirits breathed life into the first humans.

In other countries, throughout the world, there are creation stories, whether it is from a God/Goddess, some spirit, the whole pantheon making their version of humans, we hear all the myths. So, in other words, there is no single "Pagan creation story," to answer all the questions. Many of us accept the theory of evolution as an explanation for how things came to exist as they are, but plenty of Pagans also have room in their spiritual paths for the various creation myths as explanations for the beginnings of the human experience. Below is a small sample of Norse, Celtic and Native American pantheon showing the name the God or

Goddess are typically called, what that name means or stands for, and lastly what that deity represents in that pantheon.

German Pantheon/Mythology

Germanic religion, like most ancient religions, was polytheistic. In early times there were two groups of gods—the Aesir and the Vanir. However, after a war between the rival pantheons (which perhaps reflects a war between two rival tribes), the defeated Vanir were absorbed into the Aesir, and the gods of both were worshiped in a single pantheon. This pantheon had Woden (Odin) as its chief god.

Other important deities were Tyr, Thor, Balder, Frey, Freyja, and Frigg. The gods dwelled in Asgard, where each deity had his or her own particular abode. The most beautiful of which was Valhalla; there Woden, attended by the Valkyries, gave banquets to the dead heroes. The ancient Nordic gods, however, unlike the gods of most religions, were not immortal. They continually renewed their youth by eating the apples of Idunn, but they were doomed, like mortals, to eventual extinction.

The gods were opposed by the giants and demons, representing the destructive and irrational forces of the universe. It was prophesied that at Ragnarok, the doom of the gods, the forces of evil and darkness led by Loki and his brood of monsters, would attack the gods of Asgard. After a ferocious battle, in which most of the gods and giants would be destroyed, the universe would end in a blaze of fire. However, it was also prophesied that from the ashes of the old world a new cosmos would emerge, and a new generation of gods and humans would dwell in harmony.

Below is a nice table for reference on some of the key names:

Name	Name meaning	Known for/Deity of
Baldr	"Shining day".	Balder, Old Norse Baldr, in Norse mythology, the son of the chief god Odin and his wife Frigg. Beautiful and just, he was the favorite of the gods.
Bragi	"Poetry"	Bragi is the skaldic poet of the Aesir.
Eir	"Peace, clemency" or "help, mercy"	In Norse mythology, Eir is a goddess or Valkyrie associated with medical skill. . . . In addition, Eir has been theorized as a form of the goddess Frigg and has been compared to the Greek Goddess Hygieia.
Ēostre	"East"	Eostre was the goddess of spring and her sacred animal was the rabbit, which symbolized fertility. The eggs and rabbits were pagan symbols of fertility and rebirth of life and the seasons.
Freyja	"Lady"	Freyja, most renowned of the Norse goddesses, who was the sister and female counterpart of Freyr and was in .757 charge of love, fertility, battle, and death.
Freyr	"Lord"	Freyr, also spelled Frey, also called Yngvi, in Norse mythology, the ruler of peace and fertility, rain, and sunshine and the son of the sea god Njörd. . . . His sister and female counterpart, Freyja, was goddess of love, fertility, battle, and death.
Frigg	"Love"	Frigg, also called Friia, in Norse mythology, the wife of Odin and mother of Balder. She was a promoter of marriage and of fertility.
Heimdallr	"World-brightener"	Heimdall, Old Norse Heimdallr, in Norse mythology, the watchman of the gods. Called the shining god and whitest skinned of the gods, Heimdall dwelt at the entry to Asgard, where he guarded Bifrost, the rainbow bridge

Iðunn	"Ever young"	Idunn was the keeper of the golden apples, in Norse mythology, the goddess of spring or rejuvenation and the wife of Bragi, the god of poetry.
Loki	"Trickster"	In Norse mythology Loki is a cunning trickster who has the ability to change his shape and sex. Although his father is the giant Fárbauti, he is included among the Aesir
Mímir	"Rememberer"	Anglicized as Mim or Mimer who is the keeper of the well of wisdom (Mimisbrunner) located deep beneath the roots of Yggdrasill
Nanna	"Mother" or "the daring one"	Nanna Nepsdóttir or simply Nanna is a goddess associated with joy, peace, and the moon.
Odin: or sometimes Wōden	"Frenzy"	Odin (also called Woden) is the main god in Norse mythology. Described as an immensely wise, one-eyed old man, Odin has by far the most varied characteristics of any of the gods and is not only the deity to call upon when war was being prepared but is also the god of poetry, of the dead, of runes, and of magic.
Sif	"In-law-relationship"	Sif was a giantess, goddess of grain and fertility, and one of the Asynjur. She was the mother of Ull, god of archery, skiing, and single combat. Sif was Thor's second wife, and Ull was his stepson.
Thor:	"Thunder"	Thor is a hammer-wielding god associated with lightning, thunder, storms, sacred groves and trees, strength, the protection of mankind, hallowing, and fertility.
Týr	"God"	Tyr was the Norse god of war, a brave warrior and member of the Aesir tribe, he championed order and justice.

Celtic Pantheon/Mythologies:

Although the Celtic world at its height covered much of western and central Europe, it was not politically unified nor was there any substantial central source of cultural influence or homogeneity; as a result, there was a great deal of variation in local practices of Celtic religion. The Tuath(a) Dé Danann, meaning "the folk of the goddess Danu," also known by the earlier name Tuath Dé ("tribe of the gods"), are a supernatural race in Irish mythology. They are thought to represent the main deities of pre-Christian Gaelic Ireland. The Tuatha Dé Danann constitute a pantheon whose attributes appeared in a number of forms throughout the Celtic world.

The Tuath Dé dwell in the Otherworld but interact with humans and the human world. They are associated with ancient passage tombs, such as Brúna Bóinne, which were seen as portals to the Otherworld. Their traditional rivals are the Fomorians, who seem to represent the harmful or destructive powers of nature, and who the Tuath Dé defeat in the Battle of Mag Tuired. Each member of the Tuath Dé has associations with a particular feature of life or nature, but many appear to have more than one association. Many also have multiple names, some representing different aspects of the deity and others being regional names or epithets.

Below is a nice table for reference on some of the key names:

Name	Name meaning	Known for/Deity of
Dagda	"Good God"	The leader of the gods for the Irish pantheon appears to have been the Dagda. The Dagda was the figure on which male humans and other gods were based because he embodied ideal Irish traits. Celtic gods were also considered to be a clan due to their lack of specialization and unknown origins.
Morrigan	"Great Queen"	The Morrígan was a tripartite battle goddess of the Celts of Ancient Ireland and Scotland. She was known as the Morrígan, but the different sections she was divided into were also referred to as Nemain, Macha, and Badb (among other, less common names), with each representing different aspects of combat.
Lugh	"To bind by oath"	Lugh is portrayed as a warrior, a king, a master craftsman and a savior. He is associated with skill and mastery in multiple disciplines, including the arts. He is also associated with oaths, truth and the law, and therefore with rightful kingship. Lugh is linked with the harvest festival of Lughnasadh,
Brigid	"Exalted one"	She is associated with wisdom, poetry, healing, protection, blacksmithing and domesticated animals. *Cormac's Glossary*, written in the 9th century by Christian monks, says that Brigid was "the goddess whom poets adored" and that she had two sisters: Brigid the healer and Brigid the smith.
Aine	"Brightness"	Áine is an Irish goddess of summer, wealth and sovereignty. She is associated with midsummer and the sun and is sometimes represented by a red mare.

Eriu	"The land"	In Irish mythology, **Ériu** daughter of Delbáeth and Ernmas of the Tuatha Dé Danann, was the eponymous matron goddess of Ireland. The English name for Ireland comes from the name Ériu and the Germanic word *land*. Since Ériu is represented as goddess of Ireland, she is often interpreted as a modern-day personification of Ireland, although since the name *Ériu* is the Old Irish form of the word Ireland, her modern name is often modified to *Éire* or *Erin* to suit a modern form.
Epona	"Great mare"	**Epona** was a protector of horses, ponies, donkeys, and mules. She was particularly a goddess of fertility, as shown by her attributes of a patera, cornucopia, ears of grain and the presence of foals in some sculptures.
Nuada	"To acquire"	**Nuada** is known by the epithet **Airgetlám** (meaning "silver hand/arm"), was the first king of the Tuatha Dé Danann. He is also the husband of Boann. He is mostly known from the tale in which he loses his arm or hand in battle, and thus his kingship, but regains it after being magically healed by Dian Cécht.
Goibniu	"Smith"	**Goibniu** was the metalsmith of the Tuatha Dé Danann. He is believed to have been a smithing god and is also associated with hospitality.
Dain Cecht	"Swift Power"	**Dian Cécht** was the god of healing, the healer for the Tuatha Dé Danann, and son of the Dagda

Native American Pantheon/Mythologies:

There is no single mythology of the Indigenous North American peoples, but numerous different canons of traditional narratives associated with religion, ethics and beliefs. Such stories are deeply based in Nature and are rich with the symbolism of seasons, weather, plants, animals, earth, water, fire, sky, and the heavenly bodies. Common elements are the principle of an all-embracing, universal and omniscient Great Spirit, a connection to the Earth and its landscapes, a belief in a parallel world in the sky (sometimes also underground and/or below the water), diverse creation narratives, visits to the 'land of the dead', and collective memories of ancient sacred ancestors.

A characteristic of many of the myths is the close relationship between human beings and animals (including birds and reptiles). They often feature shapeshifting between animal and the human form. Marriage between people and different species (particularly bears) is a common theme. In some stories, animals foster human children. Although most Native North American myths are profound and serious, some use light-hearted humor – often in the form of tricksters – to entertain, as they subtly convey important spiritual and moral messages. The use of allegory is common, exploring issues ranging from love and friendship to domestic violence and mental illness.

Some myths are connected to traditional religious rituals involving dance, music, songs, and trance (e. g. , the sun dance). Most of the myths from this region were first transcribed by ethnologists during the late 19th and early 20th centuries. They may be considered the most authentic surviving records of the ancient stories, and thus form the basis of the descriptions below.

Below is a nice table for reference on some of the key names:

Name	Type of Deity	Known for/Deity of
Raven	"Trickster"	In the beginning, Raven was first and foremost a Creator and Trickster God — especially of the Haida tribe, who claim he discovered the first humans hiding in a clam shell and brought them berries and salmon.
Coyote	"Trickster"	This is the top trickster of many tribes and responsible for many things, like the Milky Way, diversity upon mankind, or taking the place of the moon to spy on others
Manabozho	"Rabbit Trickster"	the Great Hare is a devious Trickster God, always ducking and diving and changing shape. He has a good line in Creation, Provisions and Transformation, and is one of the most important critters in Native American mythology.
Sedna	"Innuit Sea Goddess"	She's a sinister hag with one eye, no fingers, and a giant bloated body. She is sometimes depicted as a walrus. This is a far cry from the good old days when she was a beautiful maiden. That's what being sacrificed to the sea does to you. One legend tells how she made a vow to remain single in order to look after her poor old father. All suitors were spurned and offers of marriage refused.
Manitou	"Power spirit of the Algonquin"	It fills the world and everything in it. According to the Algonquin-speaking peoples, Manitou is the primeval force which gives every animal, plant and rock their power and character. Although sometimes spoken of as a myriad of separate spirits, it is perhaps best regarded as a universal life-giving energy force.

Wakan Tanka	"The Math God"	He started by dividing himself into 4 and then back into 1, and then doubled up to produce Sun, Sky, Earth etc. Followed by branching out plus 4 more high ones, plus 4 Companions dividing the many acts of creation. The 4 Companions then added 4 Related ones = Whirlwind, Four Winds, Four Legs and Two Legs. He now manifests as the Thunder bird Waukheon who leads his flocks into battle.
Gahe	"Apache Mountain Gods"	They are seldom — if ever — seen but can often be heard drum-dancing to their mountain beat. The Gahe are useful gods to know as they can heal and drive away disease. Best contact them by dancing the mountain dance in the company of four friends painted the appropriate colors.
Glooskap	"Hero God of Ecology and Nature"	He was formed from the dust of Tabaldak's hand, along with his brother Malsumis. He's the good guy, with many tricks up his sleeve, while evil Malsumis does the dirty work. Many legends abound. How Glooskap saved the world from an ocean-swallowing frog monster. How Glooskap corrected the climate by binding the wings of the Weather Bird. How Glooskap saved the world's hunted animals by stuffing them into a bag. How Glooskap saved the world's hunters by letting them all out again. . . He even negotiated the first environmental treaty to ensure that man and nature could live in harmony. That lasted until the white man came, and now Glooskap is very cross.
Great Spirit	"Creation"	This Creator god was a mythological figure who was responsible for causing the universe to form. To some tribes, the Great Spirit was found in everything, including land, water, sky, flora, and fauna. Yet, the Great Spirit only began the creation process and then left other deities to oversee daily upkeep of the world.

Chapter Six
Different Traditions

The Wiccan religion is a diverse and decentralized religion that is part of contemporary Paganism/Nature Spirituality. Today, there are thousands of individuals and groups practicing various forms of the Wiccan religion and other Pagan/Nature Spirituality paths throughout the world.

There are many forms of the Wiccan religion. Hereditary/Family Tradition, Shamanic, Gardnerian, Alexandrian, Celtic, British Traditionalist, Dianic, Faerie, Circle Craft and Eclectic are just some of the variety of Wiccan traditions, or paths. Within most Wiccan and other Pagan traditions, there are a variety of types of groups as well as individual practitioners. Groups differ widely in size, structure, purpose, orientation, ritual practices, etcetera. There is even more variation among those practicing Wiccan/Pagan spirituality on their own without being part of a group that meets regularly. While it is true that some Wiccan traditions are initiatory, others are not.

Initiatory practices vary from tradition to tradition and include initiations by deities and spiritual helpers through dreams and vigils/vision quests, and initiations by teachers and groups.

Wicca is and has always been a dynamic religion, changing and evolving over time as more and more people are drawn to learn, interpret and integrate its core tenets into their own experiences. While there are many traditionalists adhering as closely as they can to the "original" form of the Wicca developed by Gardner, the explosion of interest in Wicca over the past several decades has led to new traditions, experiences, and options for beginners to advanced students of the Wicca. It's important to point out that even Gardener expected the Wicca to grow and change over time as people added to their Book of Shadows.

Indeed, the possibilities of all the options might even seem overwhelming to newcomers to the Wicca. But all you need to do is remain open while exploring the available options. Listen to your intuition and follow where your heart leads you. As long as you do so, there are no wrong turns.

Pagan traditions have a strong focus on ritual, and practitioners may draw from multiple sources or follow a single contemporary Pagan tradition. The largest of these is Wicca, a form of religious witchcraft that includes dozens of lineages, paths, and styles. Pagans generally do not proselytize and, while classes and retreats may introduce people to the path, the initiative to practice is with each individual. Some Pagans also participate in other religious communities such as churches or synagogues.

As Paganism is a very diverse religion with many distinct though related traditions, the forms of Pagan worship vary widely. It may be collective or solitary. It may consist of informal prayer or meditation, or of formal, structured rituals through which the participants affirm their deep spiritual connection with nature, honor their Gods and Goddesses, and celebrate the seasonal festivals on the turning year and the rites of passage of human life.

Pagans do not believe that they are set above, or apart from, the rest of nature. They understand divinity to be immanent, woven through every aspect of the living earth. Their rituals are akin to a symbolic language of communication between the human and the divine: one which speaks not to the intellect alone but also to the body, the emotions, and the depths of the unconscious mind, allowing Pagans to experience the sacred as whole people within the act of worship. The approach is primarily mythopoetic, recognizing that spiritual truths are better understood by means of allusion and symbol rather than through doctrine.

Some of the following traditions you may encounter are all of some importance in the US today. While there may be many sub-orders that I am not mentioning, or orders I have little or no knowledge of, this listing is in no way a complete one, but an opportunity for you, the seeker, to see some of the choices that are available beside the way of the solitaire who is self-taught, self-recognized or even self-dedicated. Just like there are so many differing types of tradition in the Christian, Catholic, Lutheran, Baptist or Protestant beliefs, quality may vary from group to group, coven to coven as well as tradition to tradition.

Many will try to claim to be quite old in their line, and while I am only certain of the Gardnerian line, I am not sure how far back some of these really may go, nor do I think it is easily proven or disproven that any one of them are as old as they may present to the public. I would say that the basic rule is to judge a tradition by its people and its magic: If they work and are good, they may be a valid fit for you. Below is a sample listing of some of the more well-known groups/traditions along with some of what they do:

GARDNERIAN: This is the one formed by Gerald Gardner and is also the basis for several others that are prominent today.

CELTIC: This is the most popular eclectic Wicca deriving from Welsh or Irish sources.

AMERINDIAN: Native American traditions are normally closed to those without NA Bloodlines, but these days, more and more are opening up to allow others in, and with enough already out and available, it appears remarkably similar to Wicca of today.

ALEXANDRIAN: A very similar system to Gardnerian though it is stated to be from different sources.

ODINIST: A revival of the ancient Norse religion. It is usually patriarchal and very 'testosterone filled'.

CIRCLE: Eclectic Wicca that is comprised of the best of the 60s warmth and a solid devotion to the God and Goddess.

DRUID: A century old revival in Britain that is largely ceremonial and folk-lore-oriented. It seems to be music, magic, and a tradition based on eclectic Wicca.

DIANIC: This tradition is centered on the Artemis/Diana aspect of the Goddess, with, or without the aspect of the Horned God and is frequently considered a feminist religion.

STREGA: Italian folk tradition with roots in antiquity. There are numerous variants, offshoots, and similarities.

FAERY: This is a modern initiatory tradition derived from recovered Tuatha De Danaan traditions that are described as an ecstatic rather than fertility tradition.

VODOUN: An African diasporic religion with no known central authority that revolves around spirits known as Iwa.

ECLECTIC WICCA: While modern Wicca is considered initiatory, the eclectic wiccan is typically uninitiated in any tradition, usually is a solitary, with less formal and more accessible ritual open to the general public.

Contrary to what superstitions and pop culture would lead you to believe, there are also many different types of witches out there. Not all witches are green skinned, hags huddled over a cauldron of boiling liquids, or scooting about on broomsticks with deformities trying to lay a spell on you. Nor are they some kind of femme fatale who lures you into some secret meeting to steal your soul like you see in the movies.

Today, a witch may be that 50-year-old accountant who dresses frumpy but has a few plants in their office who also just happens to dance 'skyclad' in the moonlight or maybe it's that tall good-looking guy you want to date so badly because he is such a nerd like you. With all the different traditions, there is bound to be something that fits your souls desire as far as Wicca is concerned, but just as there are a multitude of potential traditions, there is just as many types of witches out there. Now after looking at the different types of traditions let's take a look at the different types of witches one can possibly become and some of the facts behind what sets each apart in the world of witchcraft.

>**Traditional Witch-** Traditional witches are witches who have a base in the history of witchcraft and the Old Craft that came before Wicca. They take a historically traditional approach to their practice and often will study their ancestors or other folklore attached to witchcraft. Traditional witches want to honor the "old" ways of practicing their craft and will often focus on working with the local history and spirits of where they are or where they've come from.
>
>**Sea Witch-** A Sea witch has strong ties to water and the ocean and uses that element often in their practice. Sea and ocean magic will often use sand, shells, driftwood, or other elements that come from that place. Sea witches feel connected to water and ancient folklore involving said element.
>
>**Kitchen Witch-** Also known sometimes as a hearth witch, kitchen witches create most of their magic in the home or in the kitchen. They are very home-based, often incredibly nurturing, and love

to make their home a truly special and sacred space. Kitchen witches love to cook and brew and use herbs, sometimes gathered from their own garden. When practicing they combine their own personal and individual magical energy with essential oils, herbs, food, and everyday objects to create their spells, rituals, and magic.

Hedge Witch- Hedge witches practice what's known as "hedge jumping" which is venturing out of this world and into the Otherworld. Hedge witches can communicate with the spiritual world and can send messages between both worlds. Hedge witches practice astral projection as well as work with herbs and Earth based magic. But what makes them specifically, a hedge witch is their ability to cross the "hedge" aka: the boundary between this world and the spirit world. It's thought that the "flying on a broomstick" legend was a misunderstanding based on hedge witches "flying" into the spiritual realm. **Elemental Witch** - Elemental witches study and practice based on the five elements: earth, air, wind, fire, and spirit. An elemental magic is work based on honoring each element. An elemental witch may have an altar for each specific element. Elemental witches call on the elements when casting spells and performing rituals and may even have an element that they personally identify with and work towards finding.

Ceremonial Witch - Ceremonial witches have many practices, but ceremonies and rituals are practices that they hold in especially high regard. Ceremonial magic is worked into most of the elements of their practice. They likely work a ritual or ceremony into whatever they're casting or trying to accomplish. Ceremonial witches often call on specific beings and spiritual entities to assist them with whatever they're casting.

Green Witch- Also called garden witches or forest witches, green witches are highly connected to the earth and the energy that it possesses. They may have their own garden where they grow their own herbs, but they also study their area and practice with local plants and their own environment. Green witches use plants/greenery in their spells and magic. They are often very natural and love to be in nature and near anything "green"—plants, trees, flowers, etc. They do this to be as close to Mother Earth, and the spirit she encompasses, as possible.

Hereditary Witch- A hereditary witch is a witch that was born into witchcraft. It is a part of their family and/or their lineage. Their magic and practice are passed down from previous generations, though they may work with their own individual practices as well or instead of their families. However, there is still choice. Hereditary witches must be born into witchcraft, but if you do not choose to practice witchcraft you won't STILL be a hereditary witch.

Cosmic Witch - Cosmic witches are contemporary witches who look to the cosmos, astrology, and astronomy and work those elements and celestial energy into their practice. Also called "Star Witches," these witches often follow the planets and the alignment of the stars and base their spells and rituals on the different placements.

Solitary Witch - A solitary witch can be any type of witch, but they choose to practice alone rather than with a coven. This could be by choice or because they haven't found a group to work with yet. There are also legends that solitary witches are reincarnations of witches who have been practicing for generations and at puberty, their knowledge is awakened. Since they already remember and understand the craft, their need for a coven is less than a newer witch.

Eclectic Witch- An eclectic witch does not yet have one set religion, practice, tradition, or culture that they pull from. Their practice derives from many sources and, ultimately, becomes the witch's own. They may worship a higher being, or their practice may be primarily secular, or it might be its own kind of spiritual. An eclectic witch ultimately makes their own "rules" with their practice—it is entirely unique based on the individual witch.

So, as you can see, even this listing is nothing more than a small sampling of the different types of witches out there. You may be one particular type or some combination of the many already listed. What I wanted to do was showcase the different types of witches out there, that are most popularly mentioned, so you can start to determine what kind of listing or archetype you fit into. Maybe you start a whole new style, or you start out as a Kitchen Witch, but after years of practice, move to the coast and become a Sea Witch!

Chapter Seven
Sabbaths

One of the things I really like to share with our groups is the Celtic / Pagan calendar and discuss the names of the sabbats, the esbats, some of the lore behind it, and how other groups may perceive this. There are a few groups out there that will actually refuse to use names given to the Equinoxes and Solstices as they were named some time ago by a gentleman who did some poor research and got it kind of mixed up, however, since it got published way back when, many people today believe those names given are accurate.

In our Wicca 101 course, we talk about this and share that the main sabbats are named in the Celtic manner i.e. , Imbolc, Beltane, Llughnasadh and Samhain. The others, Ostara, Litha, Mabon, and Yule are generally accepted as being named that by the general public, but you will run up on hard core traditionalists who call them by the Equinox or Solstice name only, due to the one gentleman's imperfect research error and their desire for purity.

Below is a simple calendar, based on the Northern hemispheres seasons, and a short explanation on what that time represents.

Feb 1 = Imbolc

Imbolc is a pagan holiday celebrated from February 1 through sundown February 2. Based on a Celtic tradition, Imbolc was meant to mark the halfway point between winter solstice and the spring equinox This is a good time for Divination. Imbolc is one of the four Gaelic festivals (Imbolc, Beltane, Llughnasadh, and Samhain).

The name, Imbolc, originates from 'I mbolg' which means "in the belly." This is a reference to the livestock of the early Celts beginning their breeding season. After the onset of Christianity, the festival of Imbolc was tied to St. Bridget, to ease the transition to the new religion. There are a host of customs and ritual that welcome spring and say farewell to winter. Fire being a central item in many of the Celtic rituals, this one tends to focus on the hearth in your home and that also created the story of Cailleach who gathered firewood if winter was to last longer…like an ancient Punxsutawney Phil!

Some of the other things associated would be cleaning the hearth, leaving offerings to gain a blessing, making a bed for her to spend the night, making little dolls of Rush (Brideogs) or rush crosses to hang in the house. Since it may not be appropriate (i. e. . you do not have a fireplace) you can use candles which is why this festival is often called Candlemas by the Christians. Incense to use may be myrrh, or vanilla. Herbs associated are basil, rosemary and angelica. Colors are fiery such as White, red, or yellow.

Mar 19 - 22 = Ostara/Spring or Vernal Equinox

Eostre was the Saxon version of a Germanic goddess called Ostara. Her feast day was held on the full moon following the vernal equinox–almost the identical calculation as for the Christian Easter in the west. There is very little documented evidence to prove this, but one popular legend is that Eostre found a bird, wounded, on the ground late in winter. To save its life, she transformed it into a hare. But "the transformation was not a complete one. The bird took the appearance of a hare but retained the ability to lay eggs. . . the hare would decorate these eggs and leave them as gifts to Eostre.

This is the second of three spring type festivals on the yearly calendar and is a time for celebrating the balance between extremes. The growing daylight is considered to be evidence that the God is moving from infancy to adulthood. With the promise of warmer weather, the buds and blossoms spring forth, bees begin the pollination cycle, while the fields awaken with new growth. There is an almost childlike thrill to the end of winter and the coming days of summer. Symbols used are, of course, the egg and rabbit, but also seeds, potted plants, butterflies and fresh wildflowers. Herbs associated with this time are dragons blood, narcissus, jasmine, and any spring flower. Colors may be pale greens, yellows or even pinks.

May 1 = Beltane

Beltane is a holiday that celebrates springtime and the coming of summer. It is a festival that was traditionally celebrated in the northern hemisphere (Europe, Asia, and North Africa) on May 1 or May 3. It symbolically represents fire, the sun, fertility, and new life.

Beltane is the second of the four Gaelic festivals (Imbolc, Beltane, Llughnasadh, and Samhain) This was originally celebrated as a time to send the flocks out to summer pasture but before they went, they were blessed by walking between two bonfires, so that may be why there is such a heavy emphasis on fire at this time. Since this is also considered an 'active time' for the Fae folk, some of the rituals performed may have been to appease them and earn a kindness to prevent mischief from them.

Some would create oatcakes called Beltane Bannocks to eat and leave as offerings. And yes, it is also a time of fertility celebration! Think about that Maypole! Herbs associated with this time are hawthorn, lavender, and rosemary. Colors are fiery or pastels like reds, purples, and yellows.

June 19 - 22 = Litha/Summer Solstice

The gardens are blooming, and summer is in full swing. Fire up the barbeque, turn on the sprinkler, and enjoy the celebrations of Midsummer! Also called Litha, this summer solstice Sabbat honors the longest day of the year. This is translated from Sol = Sun, and Sistere = standing still, so the fact that it's the longest day of the year is appropriate. As I mentioned above, it's a wonderful time to celebrate with friends the time of the God (he is thought of as the Sun in many theologies) being at his peak.

With the Earth being the closest to the sun as it is all year, now is a time to soak up that fiery energy and let it fuel your creativity. Fire rituals are prevalent along with Spiral Dances to showcase the travel of the planet about the sun, to cultivate and deepen our connection to the divine energies around us. Some common herbs for this celebration may be vervain, mugwort, yarrow, or fern. Summer flavored colors such as bright yellows, orange or gold are best for this time.

Aug 1 = Llughnasadh/Lammas

At Lughnasadh we see the fields of corn being cut, and for some this is the true time of the festival. In the fields, John Barleycorn, who laid with the Lady in the woods at Beltane, has grown old, and now stands bent and bearded with a crocked cane. He looks to the Sun as he has changed from green to gold, and he knows that his time has come. His life will feed the people, and it is this sacrifice that we honor at Lughnasadh.

This is the third of the four Gaelic festivals (Imbolc, Beltane, Llughnasadh, and Samhain) and some rituals include pilgrimages to mountain tops or feasts and athletic competition to celebrate his mother (Tailtiu) or is remembered as two gods battling for the goddess or the harvest (Eithne). Herbs for your ritual at this time can be rose, heather, or mint. Colors associated with this festival are bronze, green, orange and yellow.

Sept 19-22 = Mabon/Autumnal Equinox

The Autumn Equinox divides the day and night equally, and we all take a moment to pay our respects to the impending dark. We also give thanks to the waning sunlight, as we store our harvest of this year's crops. The Druids call this celebration, Mea'n

Fo'mhair, and honor The Green Man, the God of the Forest, by offering libations to trees. As grapes are a fall harvest, it is time to start your winemaking! This would also tie into the many rituals involving the growth of the vines with Bacchus, Dionysus or the green man taking the center stage for the celebratory rite.

With the Full moon at this time being called the harvest moon, due to its rising at sunset to light up the sky to give more time to bring in the harvests, it is also a great time to witness the duality of the God and Goddess. With apples, seeds, nuts, grapes, and pumpkins as prominent symbols it is no wonder that some of the herbs and colors are benzoin, myrrh, sage or sometimes even pine. Colors are of course those of fall with yellows, oranges, reds, brown, and maroons in prominence.

Oct 31 = Samhain

Samhain is a time to remember those who have passed on, celebrate the end of Summer and prepare for the Winter months ahead. The Sun God and Earth fall into slumber, as the nights lengthen, and winter begins. The final or fourth of the four Gaelic festivals (Imbolc, Beltane, Llughnasadh, and Samhain) This is a time when the threshold between the worlds is the thinnest so that the Fae could more easily come into our world. The Fae were appeased with offerings of food and drink, while the deceased kin could also revisit the home to receive a Samhain meal. Some individuals may have dressed in costume to frighten the Fae away or to receive a meal, but later the church co-opted this with All Saints and All Souls Day into what is now Halloween. Herbs used for ritual at that time of the year include calendula, hazel, nutmeg, sage, and wormwood. The colors most often associated are of course black, orange, white and surprisingly silver and gold.

Dec 19-22 = Yule/Winter Solstice

Yule is when the dark half of the year relinquishes to the light half. Starting the next morning at sunrise, the sun climbs just a little higher and stays a little longer in the sky each day. Known as Solstice Night, or the longest night of the year, the sun's "rebirth" was celebrated with much joy. Bonfires were lit, people 'wassailed', children were escorted from house to house to gain gifts of spiked apples, honey, or oranges as representations of the sun, while evergreens, holly and mistletoe would decorate the home as proof of the Divine. Many of the herbs in use then, you will see today. Bayberry, evergreen, frankincense, pine, and yellow cedar. Colors are obviously the red, green, gold, silver, white and yellow that we see so often on our Christmas wrapping papers!

Please note that these are again, Northern Hemisphere, so if you are in the Southern Hemisphere, these dates may actually flip or change dramatically as your summer is not always the same as the summer of the South. As an example, the first day of spring in North America is March 19th, but in Australia, it is September 1st! So please consider your location as you may need to modify your dates based on where you live. Other societies may have additional celebration days added to their calendar such as in Japan they have the Cherry Blossom Celebration which is quite an extraordinarily beautiful time.

The Esbats, or Full Moons that come every 28 days, are used as a time of celebration, or working. You would not typically perform a serious working on a Sabbath, so Full Moon is the time to do so. While I would not mix a serious healing ritual with the celebration of a new child as an example, certainly you can do both during either occasion, I just try to not mix the two as it sends a mixed message. Many people will also include the Dark Moon as a good time for workings as well. I think it is important to note, however, that I would do things that 'start' or you expect to increase over time, during a Dark Moon as the Moon's waxing will lend its growth to the growth of your spell craft.

Conversely, anything that you want a strong push for, or you want to fade with time, are best done at the Full Moon as, again, with its waning, you can get that extra push towards your goal. And just recall that the Charge of the Goddess actually tells us to come and worship "best when the moon is full."

Chapter Eight
Grounding and Meditation

When ritual is about to begin, it's time to set aside casual socializing and focus on the tasks at hand. There will be a time mid-ritual for the sharing of food, drink, and 'sacred BS' as we call it, along with time after for further conversation and merrymaking. But now is a time for settling down, grounding and centering. Sometimes the words centering, and grounding are used interchangeably. You may ask, what these are, as while many people talk about it as if it is 'just known' what to do, or treat it like meditation, this is actually a very important pre-ritual exercise that often gets overlooked as the foundation for your preparations.

We often teach multiple ways to do this, and below is one of the ways we share. Often other teachers of the Wicca will tell you to just relax, calm yourself or empty your mind and you are ready to go. I think that may be shortchanging as, grounding and centering is one of the most important things you should know, especially since you will often work with moving energy. The purpose of grounding and centering is to stabilize your energy, draw energy from the Earth, and to bring yourself to a positive state of being. This can be done before and after ritual, or anytime you are feeling upset and need a pick-me-up. This is the beginning of putting you into that mental state of stepping away from the mundane and stepping into the sacred.

Grounding and centering are an essential foundation for your spiritual practice. It is done before and after ritual and may be done as preparation for divination or spell work. It is also used as part of everyday life when you need to bring yourself back to a place of balance and calm when overly effected by the stresses from work or everyday life. You can remove yourself from the whirlwind of stress or pressures by taking a moment to ground and center your energy. Practice, practice, practice until it becomes a natural extension of your daily life and doing this daily will make it an almost subconscious act that takes moments instead of minutes to perform.

Most often you are told to visualize (and I admit that is how the sample below will state it) but think about this as an alternative to those who do not start out as gifted visualization experts: Try to feel the results of what you are doing to your body when you relax your shoulders, slow your breathing to a steady normal pace, hear the light sounds of nature (or the creaking of your home as it settles with you).

Grounding is a term used in conjunction with the energy fields around us. Becoming grounded is about getting rid of excessive or negative energy in the body, allowing clean energy to come through. When we ground ourselves, we're calming or slowing down our emotions and getting more in touch with our internal and external worlds. Grounding our energy can be helpful when we feel either unbalanced or nervous. Being grounded also means that we're more mindful with respect to our environment.

Simply put, grounding is our connection to Mother Earth. The easiest and fastest way to reconnect is to stand barefoot on the ground – grass, dirt, sand, etc. The act of grounding was once explained to me by my sister in the craft, who is an Electrician, as a circuit that is grounding out or making that charge at the positive end equal to the negative end so that the electric energy flows smoothly. Only when you relax, breathe, and calm your mind, can you start to feel that energy flow through your body.

Think of it as your body being a cable stretching from the heart of Mother Earth to the Sky Spirit above making that link a complete circuit so that the energy can flow smoothly. If one side has more energy than the other, your electric flow is irregular and puts you off balance. You may even see or feel that magnetic field about you like we are often shown pictures of the magnetic field of the Earth, well we have that same field about ourselves that some see as an aura. If it is out of balance, your ability to push energy is weakened or restricted (think of a resistor on a circuit!)

In addition to standing barefoot on the Earth, you can lay your body down on the grass (or dirt or sand) and close your eyes. Feel yourself start to sink into the ground and draw the energy back up into your body. Focus on deep, slow breaths. Eat something wholesome and plant based. Keep it as close to its natural state as possible and if it can be organic, even better! Smudge your space with incense. Traditionally sage is used, but you can also try sandalwood or the deep, musky scents of patchouli.

Centering usually refers to our mental and physical state of mind. It's the place we know we have to get back to when we're not feeling like ourselves. When we're not centered, we might feel lost or out of touch with ourselves. When we center ourselves, we bring calm to our emotions. We do so by slowing down our breathing so that we "feel" more of what's going on around us. Becoming centered is a way to find peace within the chaos that might be surrounding us. It's about being "in tune" with what's going on. Individuals who are centered are typically, calm, and peaceful. Think about turning away from outside distractions or negative thoughts and redirecting your energy to the center of your body, to your heart chakra.

Maybe you start with eyes open, but as you gain more confidence, you can do this with eyes closed. Breathe in deeply through your nose, feeling your chest swell, hold it for just a moment, then exhale slowly through your mouth. Do this about three or four more times and you should be able to feel your shoulders relaxing, dropping away from your neck so that you can now feel your feet tingling as you relax more and more. As you gain more experience, you will feel your breathing take on a steady slow rhythm. That tingling is the feeling of the Earth matching your electric charge. You may now start to feel that tingling creep up your torso till it fills you and escapes from your crown into the sky or to drop back to the Earth, so you complete that circuit and exchange the negative for the positive energy that helps you push through the task at hand.

You can use this as an exercise for the beginning of ritual or for your daily relaxation moment, sit comfortably, breathe in deeply through your nose and exhale through your mouth till you can get a slow steady rhythm going. Sometimes it helps to close your eyes, so you are less distracted by the outside influences. As that energy climbs through you, you may feel a reciprocal energy from above that comes into you from your crown, so the two mingle and allow you to feel balanced, grounded, and ready to begin.

While this grounding below is high in visualization techniques, I ask you to not get caught up in that if you struggle with detailed visualization and focus on what you feel happening to your body as you relax, calm yourself and put your body into a normal rate of breathing. All you need for this is you, a quiet area for about five to ten minutes and a little time each day to practice this each day for about a week and I am positive you will be ready for more intense visualizations.

The Sacred Tree Grounding and Centering Meditation:

This is my adaptation of a common grounding and centering technique. It is meant to be done to prepare for spell work or ritual.

Begin by relaxing:

If you are grounding and centering as part of a spell or ritual, you should stand with your feet shoulder-width apart and your weight evenly balanced across them if you can do so comfortably. If you cannot, sit or recline with your feet flat on the ground. Take several deep breaths and let them out completely.

Close your eyes and begin to visualize:

See yourself standing (or sitting) and feel the air on your skin and the ground beneath your feet. Breathe deeply in and out, several times. As you breathe, feel the energy that surrounds you entering your body with your breath and gathering at your center. Continue to breathe deeply.

Focus now on your feet. Feel the surface of the Earth beneath your feet. Feel your feet reaching deeply into the Earth, feel them sinking down, down into the moist, cool soil like the roots of a tree, down, down they reach, deeper and deeper to the very energetic center of the Earth.

As your roots grow deeper, feel your arms extend up toward the Sun. Feel them stretch and grow like the branches of a tree. With broad green leaves reaching for the sun.

With your broad, green leaves, seek out all the energy that is you and absorb it and bring it to your Center, your strong, sturdy trunk. See all that energy gathering in your leaves and flowing along your branches to the center of your trunk where it pulses and Circles.

Where is your energy? As it passes through your green leaves it is transformed to pure, white energy and it travels down your branches and into your Center and swirls beautifully.

Feel your roots deep in the Earth and know that if there is too much energy there, if it gets too hot, if you just can't take it all that you can send it down into the cool, cool Earth and she will hold it for you. She can take everything you can give, and she will transform it into pure life energy, and you can have it back at any time.

Draw the energy back through your leaves and transform it to pure white energy flowing through your branches into your Center all there for you, right now, it is yours and you are One with the Earth and the Sky.

You are connected, you are one. All of your energy, all of YOU is here and ready to use for your Will and anymore that you need can be drawn from the Earth and the Sky at your Will.

Breathe deeply. Draw back your branches, your leaves become fingers, your branches arms but still you are connected to the mighty sky. You are once more human, a strong, capable human, focused on your True Will. Your hands ready to do the work necessary to manifest your Will.

Draw back your roots and they become feet again. No longer reaching deeply within the soil, they now stand firmly on the Earth, a firm foundation beneath you, ready to carry you about your task as you carry out your Will.

Open your eyes. You are ready to begin.

Chapter Nine
Divination

Divination is the art of getting insight into the patterns and movements of the meaning in life. I think of this as a soft magic, as opposed to performing a ritual spell, where you raise energy to affect change. To me Divination is more like taping into the energy and 'listening' to the answer to your question. There are many traditional tools for doing this: the tarot, I Ching, palm reading, tea leaves, numerology, runes, the pendulum, astrology, etc. Some of these tools carry an unsavory reputation as superstitious foolishness, others are tied in with religious traditions and are thus labeled as 'non-magical'. Multiple forms or methods of divination can be found around the world, with many cultures practicing the same methods under different names.

Some types of divination were so popular, they remain a part of our cultures even today! Have you ever found yourself pulling petals from a flower, whilst saying something like "he loves me, he loves me not"? Or perhaps you asked a "Should I. . . Shouldn't I" question instead? This is, believe it or not, a form of divination more commonly known as Floromancy! This type of divination is relatively new, dating back to the Victorian period, and its more defined methods have many modern off shoots. Typically, this type of divination is used when seeking answers regarding love, or the heart and emotions.

What each individual method has in common is that it is used to help the reader tune into their own intuition and magical ability; the mind's ability to read the movements of energy. As you will find out with all things in divination, the tools are pretty worthless without the skill of good reading or interpretation to go along with them. The specific tool provides a vocabulary, and sometimes a grammar, for understanding meaning; Much like learning a whole new language today.

Trying to use a tool without thoroughly understanding its lexicon and organization can be like trying to read poetry in a foreign language with only a dictionary in hand. The first thing to remember is that Divination is the art of acquiring answers and knowledge that otherwise would be unavailable to us. By making use of magic in its most natural state, we are able to extract information that we are seeking from the all-encompassing magical energy of life around us. Not all divinatory tools and methods are specific to future sight. Some, like Scrying and Dowsing, are methods of seeing or finding things in the present world rather than the future.

Divination is a timeless practice that, through thoughtful meditation and implicit actions, empowers us to have an understanding of what lies in the future for ourselves as well as for others. The art of divination is one of the few magical arts which has always been as it is today, and which has seamlessly existed in parallels throughout many magical cultures alike. From the first steps of preparation to meditation and finally, to the actual reading itself, we are applying ourselves to a very real task which has concrete results.

In the hands of someone who is not only well prepared but also properly receptive to the responses of the questions asked, the likelihood of a successful reading increases many fold. Divination reveals to us paths we may not have previously considered and helps to prepare and guide us to perform the right action or to properly react. Divination practices formed the earliest known understandings of magic use and its practices.

Alveromancy, or divination by sound, has been used throughout magical history and is the foundational theory upon which our usage of spell incantations is built. Used throughout ancient cultures worldwide, this was most popularly touted by practitioners in ancient Egypt. This understanding that words and specific arrangements of sounds originated in the belief that all sounds, and words had meaning. Early magic users learned quickly that certain arrangements of words could aid them in focusing their magical abilities during spell casting, and soon the theory spread to everything, even filtering into a religious belief that sounds came from the gods. In this theory, the pronunciation, and exact recital of magical 'scripts' was used to effect magical change, and it is upon this early theorizing that our current magical system came about. Simply put, the ancient peoples believed that if the 'words of power' were not properly spoken, the magic or 'divination' would not succeed.

The art of divination is not a concrete, active use of magic, as are, for example, transfigurations and charms spells. There are several reasons divination practices have such an awkward and often unreliable track record. Since there are no incantations, this staple of applied magics does not exist in divinations, so that means that each individual will find a way to make it work for themselves. While there are, throughout history, Oracles and Seers who spoke in riddles that could, in some contexts, seem like incantations - they are not. The gift of true sight often presents in the commonly associated riddles of prophecy, but this is related to our subconscious interpretation of the information received, rather than the casting of some elaborate spell.

Because of this 'lack of spell work,' everyone interprets information and imagery from their chosen medium differently. While many have tried to standardize the meanings and imagery most common to the art, it is actually fairly close to impossible to standardize a practice that, at its core, is based in the intuition and subconscious mind of the seeker. Not only that, but when the diviner is reading for another person, this additional person has influences over the way the information is interpreted - if not directly with their energy and ambient magic then by simply taking in what they are told and re-interpreting it for themselves.

Our brains love to solve puzzles and put logic to things that seem illogical - which is why we can often see patterns where none exist or find patterns in the midst of chaos. This natural inclination to create order out of chaos is both an integral part of the process and its greatest foil. Because not everyone finds the same route to the same answer, or even comes up with the same answer, often the mixture of diviner interpretation, method of divination (IE what sort of tool their prefer to work with) and emotional connections to the imagery or tool will alter the reading. Ultimately, this adds to the success or failure, depending on the individuals and tools in question. Just as some people are great with one medium, they may be incapable of using another due to it being like a foreign language and not having that dictionary I spoke on earlier.

Not everyone is able to maintain the clarity necessary to divine accurately. In order to control for any situations that interfere with the success of a reading, we must do certain things to prepare ourselves and our tools and even our area. This preparation comprises of several parts, from setting up and 'cleansing' the area to the fore-practice of grounding. Because the art of divination is based on things like intuition and the use of passive magic, it is unlike any other form of magic you will study.

Fear not; divination truly is an art and someone (like me) who has absolutely no affinity for one style…like Tarot…may be quite competent in another …say runes, psychometry, or pendulum. Practice makes perfect, and you'll find that meditative practices, or good chakra work, will assist greatly with your intuition when interpreting answers to the questions you ask. The section on 3rd eye chakra is, in my opinion, invaluable for better Divination as an open 3rd eye assists in intuitive reading of the Akashic or magical energies.

Divination works through the applied use of passive magics, or the act of 'tapping in' to the ambient magic around us. This is the 'spark' that animates us, and which exists even in the plants and earth under our feet. This magic permeates all of our world and is separate from the magic we hold internally within ourselves.

This magic exists in many places, but one of the most widely held understandings is that this natural magic flows in rivers, called *Ley Lines* which crisscross the entire earth deep under its surface in the same way that deep-routed physical rivers of water do. Though they are unseen, and certainly more of a topic of discussion for deep academics, these *currents* of magical power do exist and serve as the very bloodlines of the planet itself. Where these lines intersect, we find a 'node' or 'pool' of powers. These 'nodes' are usually used as sites for magical rituals and great upheaval, attracting those sensitive to such natural energies.

When these currents of power are obstructed, or altered, it causes disturbances in the geographical locations connected to them. For example, a forest which naturally seems to invite disaster and tragedy with no discernible reason. The Suicide Forest in Japan is one potential example of a location altered by a decaying or obstructed Ley Line, which draws from those who unwarily walk into its depths a deep and unyielding sense of loss and sorrow: in addition, the forest seems to attract all those nearby who feel these things, though we can no longer discern if this is due to the location itself, or simply the cultural knowledge that this is a place people often go to die. Dark, but there is a lesson here to be had in why it is important to learn and understand our intuitive magics - knowing what it feels like when such an effect is upon you (such as the effects of this Japanese forest) can mean the difference between life and death, if you happen to wander into the wrong place!

Similarly, to the maternal instinct that triggers when a mother senses that her child is in danger, we can tap into this completely unconscious mind, this natural magics, and pull things from our ambient or higher, passive senses that grant us the intuition necessary to predict the future and change our fate (or to help change the fate of others, of course). The Ley Line currents distribute magic throughout the world, and this is where the 'ambient' magic of our world comes from and returns, ultimately to. When a diviner *opens* themselves up to this energy, since it is at once connected to all the world and all life in it, it *is* possible to pull from that mass of energy the specific information you are looking for. Existing simultaneously in all time periods (past, present, future) this magic is both by its very nature unknowable in its entirety and filled with the knowledge of all that has, is and ever will be.

Divination is, at its core, a form of dialogue between the diviner and this all-encompassing ambient magic. If someone is reading (doing divination) for you, they are trying to enter into dialogue with that ambient magic, to learn more about the patterns and values that are presently holding influence over a person, place, or situation. The preparatory methods and the tools we use all inform our subconscious to use a particular, pre-decided vocabulary of symbols to help animate our awareness of what is important right now, of where we are headed in life, and of what we need to know.

Each individual tool has its own symbolic language, which alters the types and forms of answers we may draw. For example, the language of the Tarot is vastly different from the language of the Runes, and the use of one tool over another will typically inform our understanding differently - though the magics we draw on are the same at their core, it is the language we utilize in this 'dialogue' between us and the ambient magic around us which gives us our answers and determines how successful we are.

Some find that using a divination tool also helps them to build and deepen their relationship with their own innate magic. That is to say, the magic that is internally a part of all witches and which resides at our core. It can help you to strengthen and expand your intuition and connect you more strongly to those parts of your intuitive, natural self. Each time you ask: "What is going on for me right now?" and draw a card or rune in response, you find your own sense of things validated — or contradicted — and in that dialogue you often deepen your understanding of yourself. This widening of the intuitive magical 'muscles' allows us to grow over time and become more sensitive to magic in general.

When you pose a question via a form of divination, such as the use of cards, runes, bones, etc. to interpret the response, you have to believe that there is some intelligence in the response. If you feel you are drawing a card or casting your I Ching at random, then of course it is ridiculous to use a divination tool. What makes divination tools work is that they are not random. As you shuffle the cards, or reach in the bag to select a rune, your magic is guiding the selection.

This means that, in order for you to have a successful reading, you must first actually believe success is possible. This means you must determine that this act is first possible, and then imagine it being so, and practice this 'leap of faith' before success in divinations can even begin. This focusing of your intent and belief, or will, is what 'gets the magical juice flowing' so to speak.

This act of faith, or reaffirmation of belief, is a focusing process done before each reading. This is called many things, by many different people, but here for our discussion, let's call this process 'opening' as we are intending to open ourselves to the possibilities. You may even just think of it as a simple grounding technique. By employing the techniques of meditation, grounding and centering we can seek to open ourselves up and be receptive to the possibilities that exist around us. This is always the first step and should be done regularly to condition yourself to the process and the calm balance that comes with it.

If you feel doubt about this, then I recommend you try it for a time. After a time, you will begin to feel that, yes, indeed, there is some intelligence I am in connection with here. While it is not an intelligence inhabiting the tool, it is the connection you forge between your innate magical talents and intuition, and the ambient magic of the world around you collaborating to make information and insight available to your conscious, active mind. So, when people ask, "Is there any validity to divination?" it's like asking, "Is there any validity to any other foreign language that is spoken today?" They are just languages which your mind is capable of learning and recognizing, which offer richer or poorer vocabularies and grammars capable of certain things but not others.

They are all valid and useful in the hands of a skilled diviner; they are all crude and inexpressive in the hands of someone who is unable to understand them clearly just like any other foreign language. Make no mistake - it takes a great deal of time and effort to learn to divine with any tool, no matter how simplistic it may seem. The Tarot can often take decades, for example, just to learn the particulars of one deck and this may not necessarily mean you can read a different style of deck or bones or runes.

I often take this time to discuss how as a seeker, I was shown the Tarot as a medium of divination and was given a deck to learn on as it was considered the 'premier tool' for divination above all others at the time. Like any good student, I dove into the deep end feet first and struggled to even try to tread water! After spending months practicing and learning the 'meanings' of the cards, laying out spreads, performing a reading for multiple people each day, I thought I would never get this. We tried various decks, locations, times, even eating or drinking different things as ". . . The Tarot is so simple, how come it is so hard for you?" seemed to always be in the background.

Finally, one day, in exasperation, I threw up my hands, handed back the decks I had been given and decided to try something else. Working with I Ching, then Pendulum and Psychometry I was able to perform some simple divination. Now even more concerned I was unable to speak to the Akashic Energies we tap into due to the poor showing I had over the long months of study, I finally asked about Runes as nothing else was really working as well as it seemed to for my instructors.

When told that not many people used them due to the difficulty, I had an epiphany that if they were difficult for others, maybe they would work for me as the 'easy' stuff we already tried was not working. Needless to say, the language used by the Runes was a dialect I understood, and I was able to accomplish detailed communication that exists to this day. The whole reason for that story is to not get caught up in the "you must use this tool" but to sample many tools and see what 'speaks' to you the best.

Other cultures throughout history paid special attention to terrestrial omens such as animal migrations and weather patterns, as well as patterns of tossed sticks, bones, amulets, or rocks. African tribes have used bones in divination rituals for hundreds of thousands of years. Chinese Taoists read patterns on tortoise shells, which evolved into the hexagrams of the I Ching. Vikings consulted the runestones. Ancient Roman shamans observed the entrails of slaughtered animals. Other cultures have looked inwards for the answers (such as the

Australian aborigines with their dreamtime), or have used various herbs for vision quests. The Mazatec native tribes of Mexico, for example, used a common local herb called Salvia Divinorum (Common names are Magic Mint, Sally-D, Diviner's Sage, Seer's Sage, Shepherdess's Herb, Lady Sally, Purple Sticky, and Incense Special.) for many of their rituals and divinatory practices to aid in opening the mind's eye.

That said, even though various forms of divination have been used in all societies throughout history, the widespread use of sophisticated divination systems as we have them now, across all classes of people, is a recent development. The spread of divination systems had depended on verbal records and history passed from one person to another through stories and word of mouth. In preliterate times this was largely the exclusive domain of the rulers, chieftains, official soothsayers, priests, sages, prophets, and shamans; the leaders and decision makers of ancient cultures. Although belief in magic was practically universal between leaders and lower-class folk up to and through the Middle Ages, including primitive divinatory practices of folk magic, knowledge of divination systems and learned magic could not spread wholesale until the invention of printing. Now with the availability of books, papers and easily replicated information, People started to believe that the skill of learning to read was a necessary life skill. As literacy increased, more translations of ancient texts were made, and knowledge of divination systems was able to spread over time. Today people around the world and from all walks of life can experiment with all kinds of divination systems, including those from other cultures.

There are five systems, or methods, in particular that are rooted in history and are widely used throughout the world today:

Astrology, Numerology, I Ching, Tarot and Runes. Because they have stood the test of time and each of them incorporates a sufficiently complex and balanced set of archetypes, these are often referred to as the primary, or main, methods. While these are not the only ones, we speak on, there is such a variety of possibilities, that it would take an entirely new book to properly speak on them. Search your intuition and one of the myriad ways of divination will speak to you.

The earliest confirmed evidence of divination was on a turtle plastron excavated at Wuyang, Jiahu, in China, 7,000 BC - 5,700 BC. This was the precursor to the method we know today as the I Ching. The I Ching is an ancient Chinese philosophical and divinatory technique with a set of explanatory commentaries ascribed to the ancient Chinese philosopher Confucius.

The following is a short listing of some of the more popular types of divination known today and a brief explanation of some of the more well-known types of Divination:

Oracle Bones:

The very early Chinese Shang Dynasty rulers consulted oracle bones about many aspects of daily life, including weather, health, farming, and fortune. The prophetic bones were tortoise shells heated with rods to produce cracks that could be "read." This was the basis of the current I Ching.

Haruspicy:

The ancient Etruscans use a haruspex, or what we call a diviner, to interpret the divine/universal will by inspecting the entrails of a sacrificial animal. First the animal was ritually slaughtered. Next it was butchered, with the haruspex examining the size, shape, color, markings, and general appearance of certain internal organs, usually the liver, but also the gall bladder, heart and lungs. Finally, when the animal had been butchered, the meat was roasted, and all the celebrants shared a sacred meal.

Bibliomancy:

Using texts such as the works of Homer to divine answers. Usually opened at random or using three dice to determine what lines should be interpreted.

Augury:

Similar to Etruscan haruspicy was augury, but whereas haruspices made use of sheep entrails, Roman augurs looked at omens from birds. The practice of looking at omens was called an augurium or auspicium. The Romans believed the will of the gods was revealed by the actions of the birds. Roman divination included looking at portents or prodigies, unusual occurrences that show divine disapproval and can be expiated. This was accomplished (with or without the Senate's order) by taking the auspices.

Tsolk'in:

The ancient **Mayans** had a practice called Tsolk'in This refers to a twenty-day period of divination which formed the basis for the calculations used for the famous Mayan Calendar, which of course was a prophetic tool. The twenty days of the Tsolk'in are, however, by no means to be considered as abstract computational units. Rather they reflect the physical properties and the origin of man as well as the influence which powerful celestial beings, in particular the moon and the sun, have on his existence. Twenty is the total number of human extremities, fingers and toes, and is contained 13 times in 260, the duration of the divinatory calendar, the Tsolk'in.

This time-period (plus one day) actually represents nine lunations of twenty-nine full day-and-night cycles. As is well known, the time between menstruations is one lunation, and it takes nine of these anthropo-lunar cycles for a new human being to form after impregnation. This was also one of the earliest known uses of what would later become known as Numerology, though the form has changed drastically over the years into the modern practice and calculations we have today.

Runes:

The ancient Northmen (**Vikings**) were the first known users and creators of the Runes in modern society. These early runes were single alphabetical characters from the old Norse language called Futhark. Although this alphabet can be used for writing and has been added to and adapted over the years, these early incarnations were used primarily for divination practices and seeking answers, as well as for creating talismanic binding-runes on objects similar to what you see today as the Bluetooth symbol–A Berkanu and Kannaz rune matched together to form that symbol. The runes were carved into small tumble-polished semi-precious stones, disks of bone, wood or metal and ceramic tiles, cast onto a cloth and interpreted.

The Tarot:

The Tarot was allegedly created around 1440, somewhere in northern Italy. The earliest surviving Milanese Tarot decks references to Tarot come from that period, but this is, as yet the best theory of historians and academics. As noted, the Tarot deck consisted of a regular 56-card deck, augmented with a hierarchy of 22 allegorical trump cards. This created the standard 78-card Tarot deck. We do know, however, that there was an older version of something *similar* to the Tarot, designed similarly to a pack of playing cards from our modern era. These were, perhaps, the precursors to what we now know and use for both playing cards, and divination both.

Astrology:

Astrology was a science created around the second millennium BCE that claims to discern information about human affairs and events by the study and movements of the stars. It certainly has its roots in calendrical systems used to predict seasonal shifts and celestial cycles as signs of divine communication. Contemporary astrology is often associated with horoscopes that purports to explain aspects of a person's personality and predict significant events in their lifetime.

Numerology:

This is the belief in a divine or mystical, relationship between numbers and coinciding events. It is the study of numerical values in letters and words, names etc. Often associated with the paranormal (like astrology). As humans who long to see patterns, this is a tool that assists in the determination of the inferences that can be derived from them.

Chapter Ten
The Chakras

The seven chakras are the main energy centers of the body. You've probably heard people talk about "unblocking" their chakras, which refers to the idea that when all of our chakras are open, energy can run through them freely, and harmony exists between the physical body, mind, and spirit. Chakra translates to "wheel" in Sanskrit, and you can imagine them like wheels of free-flowing positive energy.

During our normal Wicca 101 course, we typically set aside a week for each Chakra so that we can perform yoga exercises, eat that color food, meditate daily on that Chakra, and work as an opening week and closing week taking time to do a brief overview of all seven so that the participants can actually see a difference from the start to the very end with the starting and ending meditations being the same style. All in all, this section of our course is the longest and takes just over 2 months' time from start to finish. Of course, you can read through this if you are a more advanced individual, or you can slow the pace down here and spend as much time as needed on the individual areas.

Our oldest had a huge blockage in her 3rd eye chakra when we started with her that made meditation or good visualization almost impossible for her. After a short time of focused working on her Chakra, we got it open, balanced, and free so that her dreams are now more vivid, her meditation flows so much better. Take your time and truly embrace this section as it is hugely beneficial, in my opinion, to spend time on yourself at this point of the course. In this simple chakra guide, we'll introduce how to identify when any of your seven main chakras are out of balance. We'll also summarize the defining characteristics of each chakra, from root to crown. We will touch on foods, yoga and some simple meditations.

At the very end of the seven-chakra synopsis, we will share a nice, simple meditation and even some very simple yoga poses we share as not all of us are svelte, young, athletic specimens anymore! Of course, as mentioned before, you can go online to many popular sites and find excellent meditations you can listen to, yoga information for more select poses that can challenge your fitness levels or mental training if you are at a more advanced level of meditation.

I recall thinking when I first went through my original Wicca 101 training and we got to this part, how I thought it was all mumbo-jumbo and that I already knew how to meditate and ground. How wrong I was, was a sad thing to see, as by the time we ended, my ability to not only be more flexible (Physically as well as mentally) and open to a more solid and deeper grounding was far and away what I thought was good prior to the start of this portion.

Many times, when we do this part of the class, I use a group of singing bowls that are set at certain frequencies to resonate with the specific chakra, and I am happy to say that this is also a very calming, opening and grounding meditation for many students. I also use an incense that ties to that chakra while we do yoga and meditation, so it further allows the students to be receptive to the energy center we are trying to open or balance.

Another thing we talk about (and you will see below as we discuss each Chakra) is using the Mantra as well as an accompanying Mudra. What is so special about making a Mudra while chanting a mantra, you may ask? Chanting a mantra while doing a Mudra enhances each other's effect and helps to redirect the energy back to the body to cleanse and balance each of your chakras.

Mantras are sounds considered sacred in Hinduism, Buddhism, and Yoga. You can find Mantras formed by one syllable or a combination of syllables. I am sure you have heard of people humming or chanting Om, while meditating and that is the quintessential example we hope to teach.

The word Mantra in Sanskrit means "the thought that liberates and protects." Mantras in yoga help to focus the mind. The sound and repetition of the Mantra calms the mind and stops it from wandering around. A Mantra affects your body, mind, and spirit, bringing harmony to all your being.

The power of the Mantra comes from the sound vibration itself. When you chant, the vibration of the Mantras come from different parts of your body. It can come from the abdomen, the diaphragm, or the throat. These are pure vibrations that tune you with the Mantra so that you become one to move clean energy. It will help you to direct this energy to your benefit or help you stay calm, reducing stress and anxiety.

Mudras are physical gestures made with the hands and fingers. You have probably wondered why people touch the tip of their fingers while doing meditation. It is likely to be because they are using the below Mudras during their meditation. Mudras are like an electrical circuit that gets closed when the fingers touch. So, energy circulates throughout the body. The theory behind Mudras is that the fingers are the endings of the channels of energy throughout the body.

The word Mudra comes from Sanskrit, which means 'gesture, mark, or seal'. Mudras are used to assist you and help you balance the energy flow in your body. You can use Mudras as tools to bring balance in your energetic field by re-directing the prana. You can use Mudras and Mantras to deepen your meditation practice. There are hundreds of Mudras and Mantras to choose from, depending on your intention, while some practices, like Kundalini yoga and Tantra, use their own.

A Mudra may involve the whole body in a combination of body, mind, breathing, and visualization techniques, or it may be only a hand position. We generally only show you the hand positions (see below bullet points) to keep it simple.

Keeping the fingers in specific positions in a Mudra creates an electromagnetic current. This electromagnetic field brings balance to the whole body. Mudras provide a means to access and influence the unconscious reflexes and habitual patterns. Each finger connects to one of the five elements: Air, Water, Fire, Earth, and Spirit. So, when we made a Mudra, the fingers will connect with one or more of the elements:

- Thumb -fire (Agni)
- Index finger – air (Vayu)
- Middle finger – ether (Akash)
- Ring finger – earth (Prithvi)
- Little finger – water (Jal)

If there is an imbalance in these elements, the immune system weakens, and it can lead to illness. By doing Mudras, you can bring balance back to the body. In general, Mudras are performed either in combination with or after an asana or Mantra. I find that some other groups speak about using chakra stones to use as healing or maybe Reiki Healing. To be clear, I think Reiki is a wonderful thing that you can do yourself, and there are all kinds of courses, either online, or with others in a classroom environment, that can teach this energy healing subject.

Qi-Gong is another style of energy manipulation, or moving meditation, that helps focus the Chi or life spirit to assist in healing and may be quite beneficial to Chakra work. My own Reiki instructor spent some time going through the chakras with us to insure we could open them and move energy in an effective manner.

Several friends espouse Qi-Gong, while others of my friends swear by Reiki as a way to open and heal your chakra, your body and spirit. What I know is that after several minutes of either, I am grounded, or feeling the energy of the earth through my feet like never before, so even if out of pure curiosity, I recommend giving either or both a try. While we speak of the seven main Chakra here, keep in mind that your body has minor chakra all over in the hands, feet, face, etc. that can also benefit from good studies at this point of the Wicca 101 course.

The Root Chakra (Muladhara):

The root chakra represents our foundation. On the human body, it sits at the base of the spine and gives us the feeling of being grounded. Root chakra healing and balancing fosters proper energy flow throughout the body giving the chakra system a firm foundation on which the other energy centers may function. When the root chakra is open, we feel confident in our ability to withstand challenges and stand on our own two feet. When it's blocked, we feel threatened, as if we're standing on unstable ground.

- **Location:** Base of spine, in tailbone area
- **What it controls:** Survival issues such as safety, security, and food
- **Mantra/Mudra:** Lam – Prithvi Mudra
- **Color:** Red
- **Element:** Earth
- **Stone:** Hematite

In order to heal the root chakra imbalances, it's important to connect directly to the earth. Go outside and walk on unpaved paths, dig your hands in the earth, work in your garden... These are all examples of personal connections with the earth element that will support the opening of the root chakra to a more grounded, sustainable energy flow.

If you do not have access to a garden, try walking outside at a park and pay attention to every step you make, feeling the contact of your feet to the ground. Make it a daily practice. The presence of plants in your immediate surrounding can also be helpful to bring the earth closer to you. Another way to connect with this elemental energy is to imagine grounding yourself deep into the earth by visualizing a grounding cord made of a burgundy red light, uniting your root chakra to the center of the earth. Also, another thing you can use is Aromatherapy with scents like ylang-ylang, rosemary, patchouli, sandalwood, or myrrh.

One of the things I ask our students is to try eating 'red' foods (or good solid 'root' vegetables) and to try to eat plenty of them during the week. You can try things like parsnips, red or kidney beans, red meats, cranberry, beets, or even red cabbage!

ROOT:

The root chakra is often thought of as providing energy to other chakras, so if it's blocked or unbalanced, your other chakras likely are as well. Just like a building, making sure that your chakras have a firm foundation—with a balanced root chakra—it's crucial to having a healthy, open chakra system.

If you feel controlling, quick to anger, undriven, and self-conscious, your root chakra might need balancing. When your root chakra is balanced, you have energy and self-confidence rather than arrogance or fear, and you feel calm, centered, and ready for what life brings. Here are six easy tips to balancing your root chakra.

1. **See red.**
   Seriously, envisioning the color red glowing brightly at the base of the spine, where this chakra is located, is the beginning of root chakra cleansing and balancing. Start with the simple

meditation of imaging a bright red light at the base of your tailbone. Picture this red spinning light extending down your legs and feet, grounding you to the earth.

2. **Dance.**
   I don't care if you "can't dance." Close the door and move your body. This is one of the best ways to balance this chakra. Even better—turn on music and sing along, as singing cleanses your throat chakra for an added bonus.

3. **Get on your yoga mat.**
   Many yoga postures are designed to cleanse this chakra. My favorite is tree pose. You can use your 'seeing red' visualization as you firmly plant your entire left foot onto your mat and bring your right foot up into tree pose. Keep your hips squared and your toes tucked in as you place your foot anywhere on your leg besides your knee. Be creative and make your tree pose your own. Place your right leg into half lotus or engage your core and reach your arms overhead, keeping the base of your neck soft and your elbows straight as you rotate the pinky side of your hands in to engage your triceps. Most importantly, feel supported and connected to the earth as you hold your tree pose for 5 to 8 breaths before switching sides.

4. **Take a shower.**
   This is such a wonderful root chakra cleanser. We are physical animals in addition to being intelligent, thoughtful human beings. Embrace and love your physicality by being completely present as you bathe.

5. **Zen out on a walk.**
   Take this idea of mindfully moving on your walk with you. Concentrate on your foot leaving the ground and connecting to the earth again with each step. You'll give your mind a break and cleanse your root chakra at the same time.

6. **Get a pedicure.**
   I had to throw this one in. This might be a little bit of an exaggeration but loving your feet and taking the time to pamper your physical body are great ways to also care for your root chakra energy.

The Sacral Chakra (Swadhisthana)

The sacral chakra helps inform how we relate to our emotions and the emotions of others. It also governs creativity and sexual energy. Those with a blocked sacral chakra could feel a lack of control in their lives.

- **Location:** Lower abdomen, about 2 inches below the navel
- **What it controls:** Your sense of abundance, well-being, pleasure, and sexuality
- **Mantra/Mudra:** Vam – Varuna Mudra
- **Color:** Orange
- **Element:** Water
- **Stone:** Tiger's Eye

Have you ever met someone who radiates warmth and sincere friendliness without coming on too strongly or seeming clingy? You've likely just encountered someone with a balanced sacral chakra.

Your sacral chakra is located in your lower abdomen, about one to two inches below your naval. When out of balance symptoms include—but aren't limited to—attachment issues, sexually-related guilt, timidity, emotional volatility, hypersensitivity, and trust issues. A person can act both completely disconnected and cold towards others if this chakra is under-active or needy and emotionally dependent if the chakra is over-active. This chakra is your most important emotional center and because of this, at one time or another, most of us will experience an imbalance here. So, let's look at some simple ways to balance your sacral chakra.

1. **Hip-opening yoga postures.**
   If you've ever taken a yoga class, you've likely heard a teacher say at least once that we store emotional and physical tension in our hips—hence yoga's many hip-opening postures. This directly connects to your sacral chakra. If you doubt at all the validity of this, notice where you grip or clench your muscles the next time you're in a stressful situation. It's likely your throat area (another emotional center) and your hips and lower abdomen.

   Remember also that your hips move in many directions—even though many people think of hip-openers as external rotation only. While it's ideal to do a few postures that stretch your hips through their full range of motion, holding one pose and focusing on completely letting go is a great place to start. My personal favorite is cat and cow pose, as this can be an ideal asana to hold and breathe into.

2. **Dance like no one's watching.** (You may have heard of this one.)
   Dancing is one of the best-and easiest-ways to also open your sacral chakra. So, close the door, turn on your favorite music, and move. For double the cleansing effects, get out with friends as you move your hips to your favorite rhythm.

3. **Tone up.**
   While learning to let go of unnecessary muscular gripping and tension is ideal for chakra health throughout your body, it's also important to take care of your body and keep your muscles strong and healthy. One of the main reasons to have a physical yoga practice is to make the body a fit—no pun intended—vehicle for the spirit and to prepare your body for seated meditation (another reason for hip-opening postures), and the lower abdominals are frequently an area that people let go. Some of my favorites for strong lower abs are boat pose (really hug the knees in towards the chest), pendant pose and yogic leg lifts.

4. **Visualize orange.**
   Orange is the sacral chakra's color. Imagine a bright, healing orange glow filling up your entire lower abdomen—keeping in mind that we're three dimensional.

5. **Balance your other chakras.**

    A severe imbalance in one chakra almost always means imbalances in other chakras as well. (They work as a system.) Your throat chakra in particular has strong connections to your sacral chakra. The next time you practice your deep hip-opening posture of choice, notice if you feel a release in your throat area as well. You can also try working a pose like bridge that allows you to connect with many of your chakras at one time; flowing slowly in and out of the posture as you connect your breath and movement.

6. **Let go.**

    Learning to let go—of unhealthy emotions, people, and memories—is so important. When we learn to let go of the baggage that we don't need to carry, we create space and energy for new and better opportunities. In life, it's all too easy to become emotionally closed off or overly dependent on the people around us. Learning to trust our intuition, yet not be ruled by our emotions, is something that—like many worthwhile things—takes practice.

The Solar Plexus Chakra (Manipura):

The third chakra, the solar plexus chakra, speaks to your ability to be confident and in control of your life. Think back to the last time you had butterflies or felt a pit in the stomach: That's the Manipura chakra at work. If your solar plexus chakra is blocked, you might feel overwhelming amounts of shame and self-doubt. Those with open sacral chakras are free to express their true selves.

- **Location:** Upper abdomen in the stomach area
- **What it controls:** Self-worth, self-confidence, and self-esteem
- **Mantra/Mudra:** Ram – Rudra Mudra
- **Color:** Yellow
- **Element:** Fire
- **Stone:** Amber

SOLAR PLEXIS:

Digestive issues are among the most common complaints I see in my private practice. Getting your digestion in check can be a lengthy, complex process—one that requires dietary modifications, stress management, and lifestyle tweaks. On a more energetic level, I believe addressing the solar plexus chakra is also essential.

First, some background on the solar plexus chakra. The subtle body follows a developmental path that begins with the root chakra, the foundation for safety and survival, and continues onto the sacral chakra, the epicenter of emotional well-being. These chakras lay the foundation for the next stop on this developmental path: the solar plexus chakra.

The solar plexus chakra is located near the abdomen, where digestion takes place in the physical body. This part of the subtle body, the energetic field that surrounds the physical body, is where we decide what information to assimilate and what to eliminate. When the solar plexus chakra is balanced, digestion runs smoothly, and our thoughts do not limit our potential. We can trust and act on our gut instinct and rarely leave an emotionally charged conversation feeling sick to our stomachs.

A balanced solar plexus chakra allows us to trust that there is a whole world of possibilities for us waiting to be unlocked. Opening the solar plexus chakra allows us to open up to the information we are unaware of—the things we don't even know we don't know. Once we open up to this information, the sky's the limit. It gives us the courage, the will, and the confidence to explore the unknown. A balanced solar plexus chakra allows us to trust that there is a whole world of possibilities for us waiting to be unlocked. It helps us feel empowered in our lives. When this chakra is closed or dysfunctional, we often feel insecure, unworthy, and physically blocked.

The unpleasant states we experience when the solar plexus is blocked are typically rooted early in our lives. This critical voice becomes loudest when we are at our most vulnerable, on the brink of major growth and expansion. Any emotional wounds we experience as the sacral chakra forms can lay the foundation for even more self-critical thoughts and limiting beliefs about ourselves and our self-worth. Over time, these become long-standing thought patterns that shut down our ability to imagine what's possible.

If you have signs of a solar plexus imbalance, try adding the following practices to your daily routine. Healing the solar plexus requires getting really honest about all the parts of yourself you want to change. Worthiness is not possible without bold self-acceptance. Here are a few practices to help with this embrace:

1. **Physical: Bring on the core work.**
   Yeah, there's a reason core work is so difficult! I like to think that every time you do crunches or bicycle curls, you are also burning through some of your self-limiting beliefs. So set yourself up in a forearm plank, engage your core muscles, and hold it longer than you think you can. Set a timer for 60 seconds, but when the timer goes off, stay in the pose. Every time you think it's impossible to keep going, keep going! Aim for three minutes and build up to seven.

2. **Mental: Make friends with your inner critic.**
   Make a list of all the ways you judge yourself. Include all the things about yourself you don't like and the typical circumstances where you judge yourself harshly. (Think physical traits, behaviors, weaknesses, etc.) Then, close your eyes and visualize yourself as a teenager. Silently tell your teen self that they are perfect as they are. Go through each item on the list and silently tell your teen self that all of these qualities are welcome. Thank your inner critic for protecting you all these years, then acknowledge that you no longer need that protection.

3. **Emotional: Try this mirror-gazing exercise.**
   Stand in front of the mirror, look yourself in the eyes, and say the following words to yourself out loud over and over, getting louder each time:

   I AM enough.
   I AM worthy.

I AM capable.
I AM powerful.

The louder you raise your voice, the more uncomfortable the exercise becomes. Don't let the discomfort stop you. Keep raising your voice until you are screaming at yourself in the mirror. (Note: I don't recommend doing this one in public!)

4. **Spiritual: Practice the breath of fire.**
   Breath of fire is a kundalini yoga practice that is powered by the solar plexus. It is a rapid, continuous breath through the nostrils with the mouth closed. The inhale and exhale are equal in length, with no pause between them (approximately two to three cycles per second).

Start by sitting up tall, lengthening the space between your navel and your heart. On the exhale, powerfully expel air through your nose by pulling the navel point back toward the spine. On the inhale, allow the upper abdominal muscles to relax, the diaphragm to extend down, and the breath to flow in effortlessly. Start with three minutes and work up to seven.

The Heart Chakra (Anahata):

The heart chakra is the bridge between the lower chakras (associated with materiality) and the upper chakras (associated with spirituality). As the name suggests, this chakra can influence our ability to give and receive love—from others and ourselves.

Someone with a blocked heart chakra will have difficulty fully opening up to the people in their life. If someone's heart is open, they can experience deep compassion and empathy.

- **Location:** Center of chest, just above the heart
- **What it controls:** Love, joy, and inner peace
- **Mantra/Mudra:** Yam – Vayu Mudra
- **Color:** Green
- **Element:** Air
- **Stone:** Malachite

HEART CHAKRA:

In my classes, I use the chakra system as a guide to explore the spiritual aspects of health. The chakras are like the organs of the subtle body (the energetic part of us that can be felt but not seen). These energy centers follow a developmental path, beginning with the root chakra, the foundation for safety and survival. They continue through the sacral chakra, and the solar plexus. It is not until the foundation of the lower three chakras is solid that we can truly experience self-love, an essential ingredient to an open heart.

The heart chakra develops in our teen and college years when most of us are exploring romantic relationships. It is a time when we are forced to face the painful wound of rejection, which occurs when we courageously reveal our romantic feelings toward another and find that those feelings are not reciprocated. If you want to open your heart chakra, loving others is not enough—you need to cultivate bold self-love, too.

Though there is a tendency to associate the heart with romantic relationships, the work of the heart chakra extends far beyond romance. We are not dying of heartbreak because we do not know how to love one another. We are dying of heartbreak because we do not love ourselves!

Many of us are cloaked in too much armor to fully receive love from others. Until self-love has been generated and sustained, unconditional love cannot be shared or received. This is the work of the heart chakra. If you suspect your heart chakra is blocked, try adding the following practices to your daily routine:

1. **Physical: Pay attention to your posture.**
   Most of us are walking around like hunchbacks, unconsciously closing our hearts. Begin to become aware of your posture while sitting, standing, and walking. Straighten the spine, engage the core, open the front of your chest, and drop your shoulders. Check in frequently to make sure you don't lose it and notice if you feel somewhat vulnerable in certain scenarios.

2. **Mental: Write yourself a love letter.**
   Spend some time writing to yourself. Tell yourself all the things you love about yourself. Write as if you are writing to the love of your life. Eventually, that is who you will become.

3. **Emotional: Try a meta meditation.**
   Close your eyes and visualize yourself sitting in front of you. Wish yourself the following:

May I feel safe.
May I be healthy.
May I be joyful.
May I know love.

Next, visualize someone in your life whom you love or appreciate. Wish them the same phrases of loving-kindness:

May he/she feel safe.
May he/she be healthy.
May he/she be joyful.
May he/she know love.

Next, visualize someone in your life whom you have conflict with or someone whom you find challenging. Wish them the same:

May he/she feel safe.
May he/she be healthy.
May he/she be joyful.
May he/she know love.

Sit in meditation for five minutes, bathing in the feelings you have generated for yourself and others.

4. **Spiritual: Participate in a service or volunteer activity.** Being of service is an opportunity to give unconditionally. Choose an activity that allows you to interact with others who may be suffering in ways that you are not. Being of

service is a way to generate compassion and experience how your own compassion for others affects your sense of well-being.

The Throat Chakra (Vishuddha):

The throat chakra gives voice to the heart chakra and controls our ability to communicate our personal power. When it's functioning at full capacity, it allows us to express ourselves truly and clearly. Someone with a blocked throat chakra will feel like they have trouble finding the words to say how they truly feel.

- **Location:** Throat
- **What it controls:** Communication, self-expression, and truth
- **Mantra/Mudra:** Ham – Aakash Mudra
- **Color:** Light Blue/Turquoise
- **Element:** Sound/Music
- **Stone:** Aquamarine

THROAT CHAKRA:

An open throat chakra relies on a healthy foundation in the lower chakras. The energetic body follows a developmental path that begins with the root chakra, and continues on to the sacral chakra, then the solar plexus chakra, with the next stop on this developmental path—opening the heart. The heart chakra governs our ability to cultivate self-love for who we truly are—and once we can generate self-love, we are ready to share our unique message with the world.

This is the work of the throat chakra. The voice of someone with an open throat chakra can change the world with words, pitch, and vibration. A balanced throat chakra is capable of communicating truth clearly. When the throat chakra is open, there are no misunderstandings or missed connections. In order for the throat chakra to open, the message must be so true and authentic, it's captivating.

However, when we attempt to use the throat chakra to communicate anything other than what is true and authentic, dysfunction sets in. Sometimes this shows up physically as a thyroid condition or an ailment in the throat. Other times it shows up as an inability to express oneself as they desire. Have you ever been too afraid to speak up? Do you often feel misunderstood? Have you found yourself screaming at another person but felt like that person couldn't hear you? These are common experiences associated with an imbalanced throat chakra. It shuts down in the face of inauthenticity. This is why it is so important to work through the shadows of the lower chakras before attempting to open the throat. We cannot communicate a truth that we have not yet discovered.

Language is the vehicle through which we construct our lives, thus it is a critical ingredient in the art of manifestation. So many of us struggle to create the lives we want. We are certain we know what we want and often know how to get there, yet we just cannot seem to manifest it. This is another common experience of an imbalanced throat chakra. This is the gift of the fifth chakra—it allows us to use language to initiate the movement of thought into physical form.

Physical signals of a blocked throat chakra. Hypothyroidism is one of the most common conditions, it weighs you down with fatigue and sluggishness, preventing you from manifesting what you think you desire. While thyroid medications, dietary changes, and nutrient supplementation can be very supportive, understanding the role of the throat chakra is essential. Because when we express ourselves authentically with the appropriate language, the throat chakra manifests with great precision. If you suspect your throat chakra is blocked, try adding the following practices to your daily routine:

1. **Physical:**
   Cat-cow pose. Begin in a table-top position on your hands and knees. As you inhale, arch your spine toward the ground, dropping the belly; gaze up and create a backbend shape in the spine for cow pose. The neck extends at the end of the movement, opening the throat. As you exhale, pull the navel back toward the spine, arching the spine toward the sky for cat pose. The crown of the head drops at the end of the movement, closing or gently constricting the throat. As you inhale, the whole front of the body opens, and as you exhale, the front body curls in and the back body opens. This complete movement of the spine creates a compression and opening in the throat. Move slowly with the breath for three to seven minutes.

2. **Mental: Communicate with awareness.**
   Share your current life goals and dreams with a friend. As you speak, become aware of when your language choices become an obstacle to manifestation. Notice where you are saying, "I can't," "I haven't," "I am not." Every time you make a statement that does not reflect your goals as a

reality, correct yourself. The more you practice this, the more your language will become a vehicle to manifest effectively.

3. **Emotional: Sing to yourself as a child.**
   Singing is one of the best ways to explore your voice. Singing can also bring up a lot of emotions, including shame, discomfort, and embarrassment. Start by singing only to yourself at home and choose songs that elicit a wide range of memories and emotions. Try visualizing yourself as a child and sing your childhood self a lullaby. As you become more comfortable with your voice, share your singing in public while walking down the street or sing to your family and friends. Notice the range, words, and pitch that feel most comfortable to you.

4. **Spiritual: Practice a mantra.**
   Chanting a mantra aloud is a great way to consciously direct vibration into the world. In Kundalini yoga, "Sat Nam" is a powerful and popular mantra. It means "truth is my identity." Practice chanting "Sat Nam" for three to 11 minutes daily. You can also get creative and make up your own mantra. Choose a positive affirmation that supports your current life goals. Chant it aloud daily.

The Third-Eye Chakra (Ajna)

As we move up the body, we're getting closer to communion with the divine. The third-eye chakra controls our ability to see the big picture and connect to intuition. Think of it as the eye of the soul: It registers information beyond the surface level. Visions and intuitive hits are not uncommon for someone with an open third-eye chakra.

- **Location:** Forehead between the eyes
- **What it controls:** Intuition, imagination, and wisdom
- **Mantra/Mudra:** Aum – Gyan Mudra
- **Color:** Purple
- **Element:** Light
- **Stone:** Amethyst

THIRD EYE:

If you hang around New Age circles long enough, you've likely heard talk of the third eye—the sixth chakra and an epicenter of intuition and psychic ability. Clairvoyance may be one result of a developed third eye, but this energy center is responsible for so much more than predicting future phenomena. When we open the third eye, we become aware of the big picture. This ability to see EVERYTHING shifts our perspective, so we can see our own blind spots and understand ourselves in the context of the collective. But in order to use the third eye to see through time and space, we first have to use it to see ourselves! The connection between the third eye chakra and the pituitary gland.

Each chakra is associated with physical structures in the body, so every illness or ailment can be traced to a corresponding chakra for a deeper understanding of the energetic origins of the disease. In other words, the chakras help us understand why illness develops and what we can learn from it. The physical structure most closely related to the third eye chakra is the pituitary gland—the queen of the endocrine system.

Headaches, hormone imbalances, nightmares, indecision, burnout, and lack of purpose are all common manifestations when there's an imbalance in the third eye. The pituitary provides oversight for many of the glands of the endocrine system, including the adrenals, thyroid, ovaries, and testes. Just as the third eye allows us to see the entire picture, the pituitary gland provides oversight for the endocrine system. It produces stimulating hormones that trigger distant glands in the body to perform their jobs, and its responsibilities change during different phases of life.

The pituitary gland's ability to adjust function to meet the needs of the body at every stage of life parallels the third eye's capacity to see how one's sense of self is dynamic. The third eye chakra provides the oversight and wisdom necessary to understand existence beyond time and space. An open third eye sees life as the stage it is. Embodying the third eye's expansive energy requires the maturity, life experience, and wisdom that we gain with age. It builds upon the developmental path that begins with the root chakra, then into the sacral chakra, the solar plexus, the heart chakra, and finally, the throat chakra before reaching the third eye. The spiritual awareness that comes through the development of the sixth chakra can be overwhelming for those who have not built a healthy foundation in the lower five chakras.

To open the third eye is to see ourselves fully—to see all of the ways that we play the victim, all of the ways we project our judgments, insecurities, and assumptions onto others. Someone with an open third eye is also aware of all the roles they play in the world. Perhaps you are not the same person with your lover as you are with your mother. Perhaps your behavior in some of your relationships is a response to other people's assumptions about who you are or the things they project onto you. An open third eye sees all of this, and it leaves us no choice but to move past the illusions that define our existence. Here are some practices to help you ease into it.

1. **Physical: Pituitary gland series.**
   This Kundalini kriya is a great practice for the third eye: In Lotus (or Easy Pose), bend over placing forehead on the ground, extended, and raise the arms straight up, pulling the shoulder blades together with long, deep breathing for 3 minutes. If that is too difficult, try this: IN EASY POSE, (Just cross-legged) lean forward to 60, grasp opposite shoulder blades and pull, right arm under left, and hold with long, deep breathing for 3 minutes while focused on opening the third eye. As there are multiple Kriya Yoga exercises, I will not detail them here, as it is a whole section in itself, but I highly recommend that you research them on-line to see what works best for you.

2. **Mental: Identity journaling practice.**
   Consider yourself as you are today and write a list of sentences that begin with "I am ..." Write down as many things as you can think of that feel true right now. For example, "I am a writer, I am a sister, I am a wife, I am happy, I am beautiful, I am lonely, etc." Then imagine yourself 10 years ago and create a similar list for yourself at that time. Choose another one or two time periods in

your life and do the same thing. Notice the differences in these lists and reflect on how your sense of self has changed.

3. **Emotional: Teach yourself to act through your emotions.**

   Acting is a great tool to access a wide range of emotional experiences, and those experiences affect our behaviors and sense of self. In this exercise, use your memory to elicit emotions. Focus on a funny memory and make yourself laugh. Force the laughter until it becomes natural. Focus on a sad memory and make yourself cry. Focus on a situation that infuriates you and scream words of anger into a pillow. Exaggerate the emotions as an actor does, but don't sit with any one of them for too long. Remind yourself that no single emotion defines you.

4. **Spiritual: Keep a dream journal.**

   The third eye is naturally active in the dream state. The more you remember your dreams, the more connected you become to the unconscious—where all of your blind spots live. Spend 10 minutes every morning writing down everything you remember about your dreams. If you cannot remember anything at all, spend the time in meditation, clearing your mind before turning on any electronic devices or auditory stimuli. Eventually, you will remember!

The Crown Chakra (Samsara or Sahasrara)

The crown chakra, the highest chakra, sits at the crown of the head and represents our ability to be fully connected spiritually. When you fully open your crown chakra - you're able to access a higher consciousness.

- **Location:** The very top of the head
- **What it controls:** Inner and outer beauty, spiritual connection
- **Mantra/Mudra:** Om – Thousand petals Mudra
- **Color:** Violet/White
- **Element:** Divine Consciousness
- **Stone:** Clear quartz

CROWN:

A quick primer on the crown chakra—and what an open one looks like. The crown, or seventh chakra is the gateway to the celestial world. "As above, so below" is the language of this energy center, referring to the idea that we are microcosms of a vast macrocosm. The crown chakra is associated with the pineal gland, which is well known for producing melatonin, the serotonin-derived hormone that affects our sleep-wake cycles. Melatonin production is inhibited by light and stimulated by darkness, thereby modulating sleep patterns in association with the circadian rhythm and seasonal cycles. In other words, the pineal gland of the brain is affected by the sun and directly connects the rhythms of the human body to the rhythms of the universe.

On the energetic plane, the crown chakra serves a similar

purpose: It provides the spiritual awareness that we are connected to something bigger than ourselves. Once it is understood that we are all pieces of the same whole, connection can never be lost. When the crown chakra is out of balance, we feel disconnected from each other, as well as the purpose of life itself. Depression, insomnia, and hypersomnia can be common manifestations of energetic dysfunction in the crown.

All of these states are influenced by a sense of disconnection. In some cases, we feel disconnected from other people; in others, it is a disconnection from nature or life's purpose. Life becomes insurmountable and heavy because when there is an imbalance in the seventh chakra, we feel alone and separate from the whole. An open crown chakra understands that everything is connected, and it allows us to put our shortsighted self-interests aside in service of the whole.

Think of all the instances when a driver cut you off or an event you meticulously planned was rained out. In either case the ego is furious that life is not cooperating. But what if that driver was a surgeon rushing to the ER to save the life of someone who would eventually be instrumental in saving the planet from environmental catastrophe? What if that unexpected rainstorm that derailed your plans was a miraculous end to a drought that would've soon limited access to drinking water. Sometimes a personal misfortune or failure is an integral sacrifice for the well-being of the whole. An open crown chakra understands that everything is connected, and it allows us to put our shortsighted self-interests aside in service of the whole. It transcends victimhood and isolation with trust and purpose.

While many of us have and will experience an opening of the seventh chakra, few people can sustain it long term. To live with an open crown chakra is to trust and accept all of the suffering and injustice in the world. For most of us, this is too much to bear, and we cannot begin to hold the wounds and suffering of all of humanity until we have worked through our own. This is why exploring the shadows and challenges of the lower six chakras is a necessary prerequisite to opening the crown.

Working through the lower chakras is best done sequentially, beginning at the root, where we learn to feel safe and secure while being authentic. The next step is the sacral chakra, home of the emotional body, where we discover how to feel our feelings without being overly driven by them. This is followed by the solar plexus, the epicenter of the mental body. Here we must confront the opinions, judgments, and beliefs that limit us until we cultivate true self-acceptance. Only then can we begin to share ourselves with the unconditional love and compassion of the heart.

The heart chakra is the bridge between the lower and upper chakras, and once we have generated the self-love required to open it, we are ready to move into the higher frequencies of the upper chakras. The throat chakra is a vehicle for expressing truth and turning thoughts into form (aka manifestation). The third-eye chakra sees through illusion, and when the emerging clarity is met with humility and the will to serve, the crown chakra opens up to a boundless sense of oneness and connection.

1. **Physical: Get to know your cycles.**
   The best way to experience the crown chakra physically is to connect with the cycles of the body. This may mean going to sleep earlier and waking up at sunrise for a few weeks to strengthen your circadian rhythm. For women,

keeping track of your menstrual cycle and noting the phases of the moon at different points in your cycle can be a great way to access the wisdom of the crown. Notice the connections between your body and the great cycles of the universe.

2. **Mental: Contemplate the right question.**

   The key to opening the crown chakra is one simple question: "How can I best serve the whole?" If there is anywhere in your life (meditation, journaling, coaching, conversation) where you are asking about your purpose, change the question from "What is my purpose?" to "How can I best serve the whole?" Meditate on this question and write down whatever thoughts arise. Simply asking this question activates the crown chakra.

3. **Emotional: Cultivate the feeling of awe.**

   There are a lot of ways to do this but spending time in nature is the most potent. Get into the mountains or stare out at the ocean and feel the humility of how small we are. Stargaze under the vast night sky and try to catch as many sunrises and sunsets as possible. Let nature move you with her majesty.

Chakra Meditation:

Now that you have a general overview, you can start to unblock and balance each of your chakras using some standard Yoga positioning and meditation. First let me present a generic

Meditation I have used. You can record yourself reading this and play it back or have a partner guide you through it as you wish (also there are several wonderful meditations for the grouped Chakra or even the individual if you check the internet):

> *Allow your eyes to comfortably close, and slow down your breath, into your body, relaxing your belly, softening your mind. Feel the support beneath you, connect with the ground below. Let it take your weight. Become aware of the sounds around you - let them be there. Notice the light and shade, the air touching the surface of your body.*
>
> *Sense the sky above, and the horizons stretching all the way round you, the earth below, supporting you. Allow your mind to empty what it no longer needs to hold on to, let it go, flow out and away. Draw yourself back from where you've been in your day. Draw your energies back home to your center. Ground yourself in this moment, here. Begin to sense the space around you. Breathe with the space and become aware of the rise and fall of your breath, its coming and going, the sensation, sound, slow rate, temperature.*
>
> *Breathe down to where the weight of your body rests, below the base of your spine – to your root - your Chakra of Belonging. Breathe into your Root. Let it soften and gently expand on your breath, taking in nourishment and life force energy.*
>
> *Allow your Root to connect down, down to the ground below, deep into the earth. And invite in the color red – the color of the earth. Bathe your Root with red: empowering, embodying, grounding you in the 'here and now'. Let your Root take what it needs. Chant LAM if you choose.*

When you are ready, allow your awareness to move up to your belly, just below your navel – to your Sacral Chakra - your chakra of emotional intelligence, choice, creativity, movement, and pleasure.

Breathe into your Sacral Chakra, let it gently soften and expand on your breath, taking in nourishment and life force energy. Invite in orange – the color of the setting sun, bathe your Sacral Chakra, with orange, balancing, empowering, motivating energies. Chant VAM if you choose. When you are ready move your awareness up to the soft area below your breastbone, – to your Solar Plexus - your chakra of personal power.

Breathe into here, allowing your solar plexus to soften and expand on your breath. Invite in the color yellow – the color of sunshine. Bathe your Solar Plexus with sunshine, replenishing, restoring, nurturing. Letting your Solar Plexus take what it needs. Chant RAM if you choose.

When you are ready bring your awareness up to the center of your chest - to your Heart – your chakra of self-development and unconditional love.

Gently breathe into your Heart, letting it soften and expand on your breath. Invite in green - the color of spring. Bathe your heart center with nourishment, renewal, healing. Let your Heart take what it needs. Chant YAM if you choose. In your own time, move up to your neck – to your Throat - your chakra of self-expression and personal will.

Allow your throat center to soften, expand and b-r-e-a-t-h-e. Inviting in blue – the color of the afternoon sky. Breathe sky into your throat center, clearing, opening, softening the need for control, freeing self-expression, and creativity. Let your Throat take what it needs. Chant HAM if you choose.

When you are ready, take your focus up to your forehead – between your eyebrows - to your Third Eye – your chakra of wisdom and intuition, gently allowing it to soften, expand, and breathe.

Inviting in purple - the velvety color of night sky. Bathe your Third Eye with purple, soothing, balancing, bringing clarity, insight and understanding. Let your Third Eye take what it needs. Chant SHAM if you choose.

Moving up, in your own time, to the top of your head- to your Crown, your chakra of 'oneness' allowing your Crown to breathe. Gently invite in a white light, softly bathing your Crown, balancing, restoring, harmonizing. Let your Crown take what it needs. Chant OM if you choose.

You should now feel your chakras are open, balanced and functioning correctly. You can see them spinning or breathing as you view them with your mind's eye. You are whole, refreshed and balanced.

When you are ready come back to yourself as a whole, back to the ebb and flow of your breath, back to your center. Breathe into your core. And say the words "I am whole". "I am perfect just as I am". Allow the energy of the words to bathe your body, mind, emotions, spirit so that you take what you need.

In your own time become aware of the air on the surface of your body. The sounds around you, near and in the distance. Become aware of the support beneath you. Notice how you feel. Hold yourself with loving kindness, for the beautiful, unique being that you are. When you are ready you can open your eyes to be in the here and now, to draw this meditation to a close.

YOGA Poses:

I am going to list a couple of poses for each chakra, and if you do not know what they are, or my description is poor, there are all kinds of photos, directions, courses, or even beginning yoga shops you can visit for basic instruction or assistance if needed. Please note that if these hurt in any way, do not proceed.

Root: I prefer Mountain and Garland poses.
- Mountain is just standing straight, hands to the side, breathing evenly.
- Garland is a squat with the elbows inside the knees and hands together in a Namaste position if possible.

Sacral: I prefer Active Bridge and Sphinx poses.
- Active Bridge is done by laying with your back on the floor, with your feet flat. On the inhale, lift your hips upwards while you raise your arms over your head. Bring arms, hips down on the exhale.
- Sphinx is then laying on your belly with the legs straight and your arms and palms pressed to the ground making your chest rise up.

Solar Plexus: I prefer the tall plank and Child pose.
- Tall plank is just a push up ready position that you hold.

- Child pose is sitting on your knees, with the glutes over your feet and lower your head to the floor with the arms laying back towards your feet.

Heart: I prefer the half Camel and upward facing dog.
- Half Camel is on your knees, shoulder width apart and arching your back so you can use one hand to rest on your heel while the other comes to your chest in a 'namaste' position.
- Upward facing dog is lying flat on your belly and placing your hands flat on the floor so you can lift your body upwards while your hips and legs remain on the floor.

Throat: I prefer to do Cat/Cow and Plow poses.
- Cat/Cow is being on all fours and arching and flexing your back so downward flexes are Cow and upward are like a frightened cat.
- Plow is where you lie flat on your back and try to lift your legs up over your head. This puts a focal on the throat area.

Third Eye: I prefer the wide legged forward fold and Dolphin.
- Wide legged fold is where you stand with your feet spread as far apart as you comfortably can and bend forward to allow your head to be below your knees.

- Dolphin is started from Downward Dog, then lower to your knees and forearms, interlace your fingers. Straighten through your legs to come to a Dolphin pose variation.

Crown: I prefer the Lotus and rabbit poses.
- Lotus is the cross-legged position we all grew up learning with hands on knees and open palmed.
- Rabbit starts with you on your knees, legs together and then bend forward so the top of your head hits the ground, arms back.

As mentioned before, there are several nice internet sites that will walk you through these or offer even more complex poses for the more advanced and even if these are simple or not doing the trick for you, take a few minutes to review any online items that may be more to your level of expertise. I strongly feel that a good diet, coupled with meditation and yoga make a huge difference in our ability to open and sustain healthy chakra.

Chapter Eleven
Tools of the Trade

An alter has various definitions but in our context, it is a workspace or focal point for your activity…like a mechanics workbench! Altar Tools of the Trade are somewhat dependent on the various traditions, but most will have the same or similar items in use from anything like the basic deity figure, candles and maybe some items for the elements at a minimum. Even though you follow a scripted look, no two alters for the same tradition will look quite the same as your personality will shine through with the multitude of possibilities from the different tools available on the market, your ability to craft them, etc.

    You may have storage in the alter or nearby, script holders or you have it memorized. You may or may not include flowers, crystals or personals that have a deep meaning to you, that would not hold any meaning to me. During our classes we take a day just to go over what our alter looks like and let everyone know that there is a specific set up for our tradition, but I will share a very simple photo I took from the internet that shows a very basic alter set up that I would maybe add a candle to insure I could read any scripts, from my Book of Shadows, or anything else we may have set aside to read as part of the ritual or working for that night.

What do you really need on your Wicca altar? Since an altar is essentially a physical structure, like a piece of furniture, that serves as a central place to honor deities, spirits, and/or ancestors; to make ritual offerings; and to keep sacred objects safe and visible, it can take on many forms. Some keep it simple and use a bookshelf or small table, others create or purchase ornate fancifully constructed items. It is all up to you what you want. In the very beginning, we used a set of folding tables, or TV Trays for the quarters, as well as a fifth for the main alter. Now we have a simple 'desk' like main alter that has a large plastic bin under it to store all our gathered accoutrements. We also have somewhat fanciful bar stools we remodeled into quarter alters!

In Wicca, the chief purpose of the altar is to serve as a focal point of ritual celebrations at the eight Sabbats and thirteen Esbats (Full Moons). However, the altar can also be used at any other time, such as during spell work, meditation, or prayer. Again, for many traditions, they set a specific requirement, but I believe at a minimum, you should have something to represent the deities, the four elements and a pentacle to symbolize the craft. Room for your athame and BoS are always a good idea as well, but not what I would say as a minimum are required. We ultimately suggest creating an altar as a first step in learning Witchcraft. This makes sense in many contexts.

When learning any craft, whether it be sewing, carpentry, or Witchcraft, we are well served to create a dedicated practice space. Such a space allows the practitioner to easily practice their craft without spending extra time gathering materials and finding an appropriate spot to do the work. The extra fuss can lead to becoming sidetracked and the work of the moment abandoned. A dedicated workspace also serves as a tool to help practitioners enter the proper headspace for the work.

If you always do the same thing, in the same spot, surrounded by the same objects, your mind will soon become accustomed to the pattern and quickly slide into focus on the task at hand with less and less effort. The altar then becomes a ceremonial tool in its own right. While it may not always be practical to set up a permanent alter, due to limited space, living in a public area like a dorm or condo, or practicing outdoors and not being able to leave an alter just out in the open. However, you can make setting up the alter part of that sacred space creation if kept simple with all the needed items kept in an easily totable box. What is important here is that all the items needed, maybe even your personal items like the athame, are all in that same location to save you from needing to search them out. While I would not say it is imperative you have an altar, however, having the workspace is an obvious boon to your practice as just as the other tools you acquire, it will absorb your magical essence the more you work with it. Below is a very nice example of a minimalistic alter set up that includes candles for the four individual quarters as if they were on specific quarter alters.

Diagram: A circle with North candle at top, South candle at bottom, East candle at right, West candle at left. Inside the circle: Goddess (spiral symbol) and Salt in the upper left/center, God (Aries symbol) and Incense on the right, Water on the left, Cauldron at the bottom, and a pentacle in the center. A compass rose is shown to the lower right.

Several items I would point out from this picture are that the items set on the alter also correspond in location from the quarter in question to the element they represent. Some will say the alter needs to be located in the Center of the circle, others in the North or South. We teach it to be located in the North, so that it is a focal point at the top of your sacred space or circle. Also, it helps to allow others to orient on the directions of the compass, which is obviously aided if you have small quarter alters at the cardinal points. These alters can also be as simple or as elaborate as you wish. From a color coordinating cloth and candle to all kinds of wonderous paraphernalia that mean something to you and that element.

The tools of ritual are symbolic items representing the aspects of Nature that Wiccans recognize as contributing to the circumstances of our existence, including the four Elements, the four directions, and the Goddess and God themselves. These tools vary according to the tradition being followed (such as British Traditional Wicca, Gardnerian, Alexandrian, Faerie or some other Wicca), but typically include, at a minimum, statues or other representations of the God and Goddess; one or more candles; a chalice, a wand, an athame, a bowl of salt, an incense burner, a dish of water, and a bell.

Altar tools don't have to be complicated or costly. You don't really need anything other than what you have on hand, but you might want the customary Tools of the Witch Trade which we will speak of individually shortly. These tools are as individual as the witch who uses them. But it helps to know what the basic tools are and how to use them. In the old Wicca, there are specific rules about these things. Such as a need to make your own, for it to be seen as a normal household item so as not to show you are a witch, etc.

In modern Wicca, your own heart is your best guide to what you need on your altar. But keep in mind that some traditions will require certain things or that your tools have specific attributes for compliance. Always remember that no tool should be put into use before it is purified and consecrated. A great example of a nontraditional tool is that my original druidic athame was made of wood and sickle shaped, while my Gardnerian (and current) athame is a steel blade, double edged and black handled with carvings.

But since you need to know the rules before you can break them, read on . . . There are some standard Wiccan altar tools. Let's take a look at these now. All altar tools have symbolic meaning. The meanings of these items is given as part of their Description below.

Sword

Some people like to use a sword for casting in groups. Often awkward around an altar, swords may be kept near or under it to be held in the magical aura. In the past, swords were the athame of the nobility, to show a 'God-given' right to lead. Safe to say, blue blood does not equal spiritual nobility!

Unlike knives, however, swords have no practical use other than as weapons. But with the sword you are ruler of the magic circle and can use it to persuade angles, and good spirits or punish rebellious ones. The sword is, however, still a symbol of circle leadership and is traditionally used by the High Priestess (HPs) to cast and dismiss sacred space.

Athame

The ritual knife is one of the prime Wicca altar tools. (It is pronounced AH-tha-may or ah-THAW-may.) Traditionally black-handled, the athame lives in the East, the direction that represents mind, thought, and choice.

An athame doesn't have to be metal. You can find ones made out of wood or carved stone, if you prefer. I recall one student had a very nice (about 10 inch long) crystal point they used as an athame in the Faery tradition and were quite distressed when it was frowned upon as an athame for Gardnerian use. While it's not used as a physical knife, ordinarily, an athame is not used to cut anything on the physical plane but is used as a symbolic one to cut on the astral or ethereal planes.

However, many older and more stolid traditions will tell you it must be steel, double edged, black handled and may have runes carved into its handle. Athames hold God or male energy and symbolize that. It is thought to be a similar tool to the wand. Athames are used to direct energy, typically in casting ritual circles and in the dismissing of them. They may also be used to cut energetic ties, or to open gateways in sacred space.

Boline

This is a knife you use to cut things, draw lines in the Earth or runes on candles, and other types of mundane functions, in general it is used cut physical things such as herbs when harvesting or cloth for sachets, poppets, or whatnot. Traditionally the working knife is white handled, single edged, sharp. This knife is usually distinct from the Athame, which is a symbolic knife only, and not used for other purposes by most witches. Not all witches count the working knife as one of their altar tools, but just a functional implement that may be used inside and out of sacred space.

Wand

The wand is like a portable, handy version of a broom which is sometimes called a Besom. There is a theory that originally one instrument performed all the purposes served by the two today. A wand can be made of any natural material. Wood is traditional. Since all woods have unique Powers, you may like to choose the wood to suit your particular needs.

Wands can be used for divination and channeling magical energy. They can be used to cast and dismiss circles, in place of the athame. It is used in a gentler manner than the less subtle and decisive athame. The wand is typically shorter than 12 inches, made of wood like Oak, Hazel, Elder or Willow for its ties to nature and air, often somewhat phallic, but often you may see them made from crystals or some combination of the two. The magical wand goes in the South, for the power of will, magic, and transformation. It is a symbol of the god, air and in some traditions fire, energy.

Chalice

The chalice or cup is one of the most important altar tools. It signifies the Mother Goddess and the element of water. This can be anything from a simple wine glass to some fanciful bejeweled goblet. A cup or wine-type glass of any material, except maybe plastic, will do, or even a bowl. Something that holds water and, ideally, is round or curvy is good. Silver is always nice for Goddess tools - a silver chalice is a perfect Wiccan chalice but do be aware that wine can be corrosive to the metal and this material may be better served as a libation cup.

The Chalice is typically used for ceremonial drink, offering libations to the Divine or holding the salt-water solution if no elemental bowls are used. We have a very beautiful goblet made of turned wood currently that replaced a ceramic vessel we had for several years. I think if we were to replace this one at some point, a nice glass, low stemmed 'red wine' styled goblet may be used as the next alternative with some etched symbols added to differentiate it from the mundane for us.

Pentacle

The Pentacle, a 5-point star within a circle, usually is placed in the center of the altar. The pentacle is also one of the most important altar tools, offering protection and power in magical work. This is also a symbol of the Goddess. It also represents the four elements of air, fire, water, and earth, with the fifth element of spirit, combined in a sacred circle to bind them together. You may actually find this symbol inscribed on the hilt of an athame, upon the doorways of homes for protection, or drawn in the air during ritual to add power to the working or calling of the elemental quarters. These are typically made of anything from cloth, wood, stone or even metals and placed upon the alter as a middle point where blessing of other tools can start.

Cauldron

Aside from the broom and the wand, the cauldron is possibly the most iconic symbol of the Witch in the imagery of today's popular culture. The origins of this association come to us from ancient Celtic myth, where cauldrons appear in connection with many magical transformations. In particular, there are several stories that feature the Dagda, who possessed a magic cauldron that was always overflowing with food and could never be emptied. Traditionally cast iron, a cauldron is like a 3-legged rounded cooking pot. You can get them in sizes from tiny to huge. They are a symbol of the creative force of transformation and obviously associated with the element of water and as its round shape suggests also of the Goddess.

Cauldrons are handy items for burning things, like incense and herbs or for the brewing of oils or potions. This is one of the reasons it is one of the most common Wiccan tools but because of this many see it as not a necessary item that must be on the alter.

Bell

While the purpose and meaning of bells varies widely among many different traditions, it's generally recognized that the ringing of a bell communicates a message of some kind, whether to participants in the religion or to entities in the spirit world. For some, bells are like the Voice of the Goddess. The bell is usually a symbol for the wiccan practice itself, however. When you ring one, it brings the Divine's attention to you. Also, your attention to the Divine! We often use it at the very start of our rituals as an act of attention.

A bell with a lovely tone will call beautiful, healing energy to you, while the sound of one may also banish or clear excess or negative energies. At the end of a ritual is a good time for this, but if unwanted energy crops up during a ritual, you can use the bell to disperse it. I once took part in an energy working workshop and at the end of the course, the group of about 14 individuals had raised a serious amount of energy so that the room fairly hummed with it. You could feel it crawling along your skin like some mild electric current, causing hair to stand out. The instructor had a large gong in the room and struck it three times forcibly and the room was immediately cleansed of all the energy making each of us let out a small sigh as the amount that had built up was released.

Candles — Direction Candles, God, and Goddess

As we talked briefly above on Quarter Alters, candles are used to invoke and hold the Powers of each Direction/Element or Guardian. I like to keep it simple at the very beginning for these and just have a small alter for the four cardinal points of the compass that is just a corresponding color of cloth and candle. I prefer unscented, but I know that some people like to have a scent that corresponds to that cardinal point as well. So, in my case, one candle for each of the directions, color-coded, with a cloth on the altar.

One would go in each appropriate direction . . .

> **For North:** green, maybe a pine scent if you prefer
> **For East:** yellow with a lavender scent if you like
> **For South:** red with a cinnamon or warm spice is nice
> **For West:** blue with an ocean breeze scent ties it together

Candles - God and Goddess Candles

Often large candles, such as pillar candles, are used to represent the God and the Goddess. These are usually set on either side of the Pentacle, or somewhere in the center of the altar. Other options are having just one large candle for the Great Spirit, or three - white, red, and black - for the Maiden, Mother, and Crone or two white and a red in the center for the same grouping. Where they go is up to you. Somewhere they won't drip onto delicate items or catch things on fire is always good. These candles invoke the Energies of the Divine.

Deities

Images or representations of any Gods and Goddesses who are special to you are always welcome on an altar. Though of course we could not respectfully consider them "altar tools." They are more than reminders of Divinity. Statues of the Gods and Goddesses can actually hold the vibrations of the Divine. So, your altar becomes a living temple - a place where the

Divine dwells. I have seen simple little clay items all the way up to elaborate brass statues that cost a small fortune being used for this. As with anything else we have spoken on, this is based on your tradition, your own heart, practices, or even needs of the moment as you may select representation for the current Sabbat or the Esbat you're working at this time.

Scourge

The scourge is a small whip or cat of nine tails type of instrument that is used as a sign of power or used for purification. You may recall watching movies or reading about postulants performing self-flagellation in an attempt to purify the soul? Sometimes it can be used to assist in raising Kundalini energy prior to the Great Rite. Some say you must suffer to learn.

Libation Dish

A small dish, bowl, or cup can go in the center, ready to receive offerings for the gods and goddesses. You can also use your altar chalice or cauldron for this purpose. Later, after finishing the ritual, you can pour or bury the offerings in the Earth, or into living water to carry them to the Divine.

Offerings

When you would honor the Divine with a gift of thanks or prayer, you can bring them to the Altar as an offering. Often flowers are kept on the altar as an offering. Anything that is beautiful or special to you, or symbolic of the purpose for the offering, can be used. Some people will make offerings from their cakes and wine portion of the ritual that is added to the libation cup.

Altar Cloth

An altar cloth is optional, but useful. By choosing one with an appropriate color or design, you set the stage for the energy of your altar. It's also handy on a pragmatic level. It keeps dripping wax from marring your altar top. And since dripping candles are a hazard common to all witches, you may want to choose a cloth that isn't too hard to remove wax from. Or it is so expensive you will cry if it gets ruined. As spoken on above, these can be changed out for the Sabbat to help create the mood or as a visual queue to the energy being raised. We currently have a whole plethora of Altar clothes that we use for each Sabbat or during the individual esbats or special rituals we perform.

Salt and Water

A small bowl of water with another for salt can represent the elements of Earth and Water. These can then be used (once salt is added to the water) for cleansing. Water and salt are both purifying agents, not only in the physical realm but the spiritual as well. Salt water also represents the energies of earth and water united, the ocean womb which gave birth to all life on the planet. While this may seem an insignificant addition to your altar tools, it holds great power.

Scent (incense) and Fire (or a candle)

Some representation of air, commonly something scented like incense, essential oils, or smudges, or else a flying bird's feather goes in the East, to represent Air. Sacred scents are used to cleanse an area energetically, call in certain powers, or help witches shift consciousness. Feathers can also be used to cleanse energy fields, and to fan incense or smudge smoke. Put an incense charcoal in the bottom and sprinkle the herbs and powders onto it for incense. Also, as a representation of Fire, you may use a specific red candle, so you now have all four of the Elements represented on your alter. Once this is blessed, just like the water and salt combo, you can use this to cleanse the circle or participants prior to creating the sacred space.

Book of Shadows

If you have a Book of Shadows, it should be kept on your altar, preferably. If your altar is not private enough, or you can't keep it there for another reason, then keeping it under your altar is best. If you have other books that you use for reference for spells or rituals, it may be handy to keep them nearby as well. It's better to have them within the cast circle than to leave the circle to look up something.

Remember the Witch's Silver Rule. And now, having said all 'this-goes-here' and 'that-does-that,' I would like to reiterate that you can have a powerful and lovely altar without following any rule but one: Do What Feels Right! If you don't enjoy it and find it meaningful, if it doesn't carry the energy you want - whether peaceful or stimulating or charged with power or anything else - the Divine will not find it as such either. Make it to please yourself, and you will please the gods as well.

Altar tools are symbols, so please remember this one thing: It is the **meaning and energy** we invest in them that gives them their power. Listen to your heart; it's the seat of your Power. If something else would be a better symbol for you than what's listed here, it is probably wise for you to use it.

Choose What Suits Your Soul, because in all cases, it's inadvisable to use a tool that you have a negative association with. For instance, if knives make you think of violence first and foremost, then find an alternative for an athame. If the phallic likeness of the wand is too much for you, get one that is more like those used in the Harry Potter movies.

Many witches use items that are especially important to them as their athames, wands and so forth that do not meet the standard traditional requirements – I remind you of the one individual who used a lovely long crystal point as an example once again.

Since there is no set way to create your alter, and in some cases your other tools, there are many ways to go about doing this. Some will buy everything from the internet, the local occult shop. Others may be quite crafty Do It Yourselfers and make everything on their own! I am pretty sure that most of us are somewhere in between those extremes. You may use alter clothes to change out for the seasons, the quarters or use the same one always. Just as you may 'upgrade' your personal Accoutrements from time to time. What is important above all else is your intent for this to be sacred and that you work with it routinely so that it absorbs your spiritual energy as well as becomes that focal point for your worship and work.

Chapter Twelve
Energy and Magic

What constitutes basic energy work varies from one place to another, or even from person to person. There are wide-ranging opinions on what *magical energy* is let alone when and where it's needed, and how to "raise" or access it, etc. Rather than try to address them all, the following examples will suffice as a starting point for defining what magical energy is in the context of these exercises.

Some people will tell or describe a variety of visualizations in which you are holding your hands over an object while visualizing a "a dim bluish light hovering over it." Others may tell you to visualize a "glowing bluish light" emanating from the tip of your athame while tracing the summoning or banishing pentagrams some groups may use during rituals in the air, so that they end up leaving a blue-flame pentagram hovering at each quarter of the circle.

Another place you might have encountered the concept of magical energy was the *Cone of Power* exercise (or meditation), famously described by Starhawk in her important work heading into the 1980s, The Spiral Dance. It's something of a group meditation with many variants, often included in circle casting or practical working. In every case the Cone of Power was classified as "energy raising."

This typically is taught as the group starts to create this energy by everyone standing in a circle and holding hands to start. A leader speaks out a guided meditation that included everyone imagining they have roots stretching to an infinite pool of energy deep in the earth. On cue, everyone draws the energy up to ground level, then spin it around the circle to form a cone, and on from there.

Aside from the concept of "energy," the thing all of these examples have in common is a demand to visualize or imagine the energy. There was and still is a common 'fake-it-till-you-make-it' principle among many even today. I have heard it many times in different settings through the 80s and 90s and even in the 2000s: "If you believe in it and act as if it is real, one day you'll find that it has become real to you." This charlatan response of commonality speaks to its effectiveness for many.

However, the 'act as if' approach doesn't work for everyone. One reason may be that some people aren't natural visualizers. But thankfully we as humans have more going for us in our SIX senses. Yes, I said six. Hearing, Seeing, Tasting, Feeling, Smelling and my favorite is the least used. . . Common. It's important to note that the ability to form mental images probably isn't a simple yes/no issue for most people. We're probably all somewhere along a continuum. That means that people who just can't seem to do it at all, are at one extreme and super-visualizers are on the other, with the rest of us 'normal' middle ground folk, scattering the ranges between.

Like so many of you who have experience with this section of Paganism, I was taught from the get-go that visualization was the key...or to fake it till I make it... and actually in our last few classes have had to stop people from trying to jump ahead on the "energy ball" exercise from immediately jumping into the visualization of a small glowing bluish energy ball like they are 'Star lord' learning for the very first time to play catch with dad! The following instructions were developed to provide a process by which people on the lower end of that spectrum can develop the ability to sense and control (to a degree) the sensations of magical energy, not as an imagined phenomenon, but as a real sensory process. As might be expected, there is no visualization involved in this section of the story.

Leaving the theory aside for present purposes, these instructions assume that the experience of magical energy is a real (not in any way imaginary) perceptual experience of your personal space, the area immediately around your body. Given that we do so much of our interacting with the world in that space, it shouldn't be a surprise that we have specialized perceptual systems to facilitate that. It's how we hit the mark when we reach out to shake someone's hand, for example, or seat a screw on a screwdriver.

Starting from a technical stance of personal space perceptions, an astute observation I developed was that the key to sensing magical energy wasn't *'visualizing'* the energy, it was focusing my attention on the area where the energy was supposed to be. That is, after all, what good visualizers are doing when they visualize magical energy. So instead of asking people to visualize, my instruction to the aspirant is to focus their attention in this manner. This innovation has proven useful for many who have been frustrated by the more common instructions available.

The first steps of the Basic Energy Work sequence are, of course, designed to give you, the poor visualizer, a fighting chance to learn energy work in its most basic form. This relies on your sense of feeling, smell, hearing and to some very small degree your ability to visualize… BUT that is the end goal more than the starting skill you are expected to have.

Now before you begin the exercises below, is a good time to remind you of the Chakra work we did earlier. You may recall that besides the main seven chakra along our main torso is a multitude of other chakra in your hands, feet, face, etc. There are smaller chakra all along your body and you can use your already gained expertise on them to your advantage now. If when you place your hands together to feel the heat or crackle of energy and do not feel anything at all, it may be due to having closed chakras in your palms.

You can do one of two quick actions to 'open' them before beginning the exercise. The first is to hold your hands in front of you with the backs almost touching. Open and close them both about 3 times and then switch the position of the hands from top to bottom and open and clench them again another three times. You should now have opened the palm chakras so you can begin. If that one does not work for you, you can try the old "Mr. Miyagi" approach of slapping the hands together and then vigorously rub your palms back and forth for a few seconds. I am almost positive you will now feel a tingling between your palms!

The Basic Exercise:

The base assumption of this exercise is that the sensations of magic energy are a real perceptual experience that primarily depend on how and where you focus your attention. The rule is: if you can focus your attention in the right way, you'll feel it as a physical sensation. It won't be as prominent or distinct as a physical touch on your skin, but it will trigger your touch-like perception.

Tuck your elbows into your sides so that you can comfortably extend your hands away from your body at a perpendicular angle. Turn your palms to face one another. Hold them flat about a half inch apart.

Take a few deep breaths and relax. Then focus your attention on both palms at the same time. Many people develop subtle sensations in their palms within a few seconds. The sensations are usually quite subtle, to the degree that, if sensed under normal circumstances may not be noticed at all or might simply be dismissed as unimportant. The purpose here, however, is to intently focus attention on those sensations no matter how faint. For most people, the sensations naturally become more intense with the added attentional focus. This can feel like your palms are tingling (like when a limb 'falls asleep') or even may feel like little static shocks all along your palms. You may even feel heat or cold.

When sensations in both palms are present, increase the space between your hands as the space you are focusing on. Some people describe a flow or a circuit between the hands within a few days of practice. That is essentially the aim, but don't fool yourself about it. Feel it if you do and don't feel it if you don't.

Maintain whatever level of sensations you get for as long as desired. When satisfied, relax your hands, take in a deep breath, and as you exhale gradually turn your palms upward as you slowly separate them. Let your hands come to rest in your lap if seated, at your sides if standing. The sensations in your palms will quickly diminish to insignificant, as the energy dissipates.

The goal from the beginning is to do 5 minutes or so twice a day, increasing as the sensations intensify. After two weeks or so of satisfactory results, move on to the next step. Importantly, if after two weeks of the daily work above you don't experience any sensations at all, or nothing has changed, these instructions may not be for you. Assume the fault is in the instructions rather than in yourself. That's what I think.

Simple Energy Manipulations

Initiate a basic flow of energy between your palms following the steps of the basic exercise.

When the energy feels stable enough, keep your palms facing each other but move them to manipulate the energy into a ball about 6 inches in diameter. While there are many ways to accomplish this goal, a common way is to curve your fingers in slightly and move your hands in a manner like that of forming a snowball. The outer surface of a ball would be smooth and uniformly spherical, but don't expect that of your energy ball. It's more likely to be a constantly morphing blob with something of an aura about it, which you'll also be able to feel with practice. However, it feels, try to contain it as best you can.

The sensations in your palms are expected to change

somewhat during this exercise but should not significantly diminish as long as your attention is properly focused. It's more likely to feel more intense once the novelty wears off. If the sensations do seem to diminish or you lose focus, you can bring your hands back into their original alignment and start over.

Continue the exercise as above twice a day for 5 to 10 minutes until you begin to feel some level of mastery.

Extended Energy Manipulations

Manipulation 1

Initiate a basic flow of energy between your palms and form an energy ball.

When the energy ball is relatively stable, slowly pull your hands slightly apart while leaving the ball in its original size and location. The sensations in your palms are likely to change with distance from the ball but you should continue to feel connected to the energy ball through your palms while they face the energy mass. It's not uncommon for the energy mass to expand when performing this action, but your goal is to keep it the same size as it was between your hands.

After a few moments, bring your hands back inward to cup the ball in front of you. Repeat steps 2 and 3 as many times as you like.

Manipulation 2

With the energy between your palms in original position, turn your palms to face upward, allowing the energy ball to hover in front of you just above your palms. Then keeping your palms in place, move your attention upward to lift the energy mass about 3 inches above the left palm. The sensation in your palms is likely to change, but you should continue to feel connected and in direct control of the energy.

Remember, the key to accomplishing this task is where your attention is focused. Now try to move the ball to be over your right palm about 3 inches above it. Once you have done this, bring the ball back down to its original place. Practice this step as many times as desired moving the ball from one palm to the other.

Cup the energy ball in your hands again.

When you feel satisfied with the session, take in a deep breath, and as you exhale gradually turn your palms upward as you slowly separate them. Let your hands come to rest in your lap if seated, at your sides if standing. The sensations in your palms will quickly diminish to insignificant as the energy dissipates.

Continue to work on these exercises till you begin to feel some level of mastery.

Final Thoughts

If you spend three months doing these daily exercises, you'll be well-prepared to move on to more Advanced Energy Work. What most people learn is that the sensation of magical energy is indeed a physical sensation, but that they're subtle enough to ignore while going about the things we do every day. Taking the time out to focus attention acutely and sustaining attention on the space near the body really is enough to feel these subtle sensations for what they truly are. Then, the ability to shape and somewhat control the source of the sensations suggests new worlds of possibility. Also realize that by feeling the energy between your hands, you started to maybe see or smell it while some people actually hear it like a crackling of milk over popped rice.

If you have done the Core Chakra work, we discussed earlier, your core chakra should be opened, aligned, and balanced to some degree, which will even facilitate your ability to sense, feel or manipulate the energy you are working with.

Cone of Power Exercise

Sooner or later, you may work with a group that wants to charge something or to impart power into a spell that goes out into the Akashic or spirit world. Maybe you work as a solitary and have a need to generate and manipulate as large a quantity of energy as you can. We often gather everyone in the class together for this as opposed to making the energy manipulation exercises above homework.

We start with all sitting or standing in a circle. We then perform a simple ground and center exercise. Standing or sitting in a circle, take hands. Begin with a Group Breath, and gradually build a wordless Power Chant. You may make a growling noise, or a reverberating intonation. Alternately we have used a mantra for a chakra like OHM that is vibrationally intoned with a deep resonance.

What matters is you are not clapping, shouting, or chaotically making noise, but using a focused oral sound that vibrates in your body in an increasing manner. If in a group, you can have one person lead this while the others join in, or if solo, you can use this and 'feel' the energy build creating a higher level building up on the last in a higher towering force. As the energy builds, visualize it swirling clockwise around the circle. See it as a blue-white light. It spirals up into a cone form – an upright shell, a cornucopia. Hold the visualization until it glows. If you still struggle with visualization, you should feel your skin tingling as the energy levels increase. You may feel this electric charge climbing up your body and even moving above you.

The energy forms we build have a reality of their own. As the power rises, people will intuitively sense the form that takes shape. As the peak is reached, the chant becomes a focused tone. If you have an image that represents your intent for the working, focus on it. Sometimes words or phrases come through. let the power move until it falls, this usually happens suddenly rather than gradually. Releasing this amount of energy for the first time can be quite the experience, and may leave you somewhat fatigued, but accomplished. Let the energy go, fall to the ground, if need be, and relax completely, allowing the cone to fly off to its objective. Breathe deeply and let the residue of power return to the earth, for her healing.

The last thing I like to show people is that it is not always a static exercise to move energy. In our class we also try to show 3 or 4 Tai Chi / Qigong steps to move energy and increase flow so that the students can have a completely different experience. Does this work for everyone? No, but I believe that people learn in many different ways and by showing you as many different way to do something, we may hit on the way that works best for you. As usual, I will attempt to demonstrate via the written word how to perform these steps, but just like the yoga we looked at above, please feel free to look some of this up on the internet or seek out a teacher in your area. Also, as always, if it hurts, don't do it!

I am increasingly interested in therapies and activities that work on an energetic level in my body and did a short course in tai chi chuan on the advice of a friend. Usually referred to as simply tai chi, this is an ancient non-competitive Chinese martial art that originated in ancient China. A martial art it may be, but it's a soft one - there are no belts or levels, and the emphasis is on balancing the body and mind rather than on combat like some other Kung Fu styles do.

In practice, tai chi is a moving meditation combining slow, gentle, graceful movements with the breath to stimulate chi. Also spelt qi, this is the Chinese word for the life force or vital energy of the body and the universe. Known as ki in Japanese and prana in Sanskrit, chi flows through channels called meridians in the body. It's when these get blocked that health problems occur and by encouraging the energy to flow freely helps calm the mind, keep the body supple, reduce stress and improve circulation - just like yoga or therapies such as shiatsu and reiki do from the other various groups we have spoken of as well.

There are various forms, and a whole series of moves which can take years to perfect in their entirety. The basic form is a continuous sequence of movements with 24, 48 or 108 steps. I confess I felt a little silly at the beginning, moving with my knees bent and apart, pretending to hold my invisible ball of energy or making it flow from one open hand to another. However, once I got the hang of it, I found it a liberating, dance-like practice, which really helped to calm me down.

At the heart of tai chi or Qigong is a belief in the Taoist philosophy of yin and yang, the primal opposing but complementary forces said to be found in all natural things. Yin is an expansive, relaxing, cooling, female force, while yang is a contracted, energetic, heating, male force, and for a healthy body and mind you need to get a balance between the two. Chinese therapists will tell you that unhealthy yang qualities can include lots of tension, stiffness in the body, a loud voice, and a stubborn, aggressive, obsessive personality. By contrast, an unhealthy dose of yin may see you low in energy, with a quiet voice, under confident, overly sensitive, and untidy. From an Asian spirituality stance, this is balanced and, to me, a similar outlook to how Wiccans embrace the duality of the Lord and Lady as part of daily life.

A related practice is qigong, a Chinese exercise regime based on similar principles which uses breathing and movement to develop a strong chi. At its core is the art of wuwei - letting go of habitual striving through simple movements and standing postures. I'm all for anything that helps us to let go of our striving - and what's good about both these activities is that they're suitable for people of all ages and levels of fitness. They don't need lots of equipment, but are usually practiced in light, loose fitting clothes and socks or bare feet.

An increasing number of spas and retreats offer tai chi or qigong as part of their exercise programs. These are especially good to take if you've only got time for a one-off session. As the basic movements are simple to grasp, you'll be able to have a relaxing, in-the-moment experience rather than spending the time "learning" something complicated. Like yoga, they are also easy to practice at home, even if you just do a few moves each morning. Let's get started with a few examples just like we did for the chakra yoga. Most training sessions start with the standard exercise:

Awakening the Qi

Stand calmly and relaxed so that the toes point forward. Keep your knees slightly stretched or bent. Let the whole body hang slightly and stretch your hands vertically away from you with the palms up. Start at the lower level of your pelvis and pull your hands slowly upwards and slightly outwards so it looks like a "T".

At a certain height (about shoulder height), turn your palms so that your palms are now downward facing and let them slide gently and slowly back down to the pelvis. I like to inhale on the lift and exhale on the drop to move breathe and energy at the same time.

MaBu (Horse Stand)

Qigong without MaBu doesn't work. This pose is one of the best for beginners because it trains both: mind and body.

First, take a broad posture and lower your hips to the knee level. Your back should remain straight. Make sure your ankles are at 90 degrees to your shin and your knees are at 90 degrees to your leg and shin.

Now turn your feet outwards, about 45 degrees. The hip remains stretched out in a straight upward position. Ideally, "pull" your back a little behind your shoulders.

Point your head forward and stretch out your hands directly in front of you. Bend your elbows behind your shoulder so that your hands are at the height of your lower chest. The two index fingers should point upwards while the remaining fingers are relaxed. Breathe in and out deeply for several breathes to clear the mind and relax the body.

Keep this position for about 10 to 30 seconds.

This will stretch and strain your thighs somewhat so remember to hold it only as long as you can but try to push yourself for more each day.

Lifting the Sky

Place your hands slightly below your navel, with your palms facing the ground. Then lift them slightly up to your head. There you turn the palms away from each other and let them slide slightly downwards towards the navel again until they are back in their starting position. This position is similar to the first except instead of a lifting your arms up and down, you are moving in a circular action, and you should focus moving the energy up and down through your body as you breathe in and out. Sometimes it also helps if you imagine that you make a small circle pulling energy upwards as you inhale and lift your hands then exhale as you lower them back down to the starting position.

Separating the Clouds

Start in a shortened MaBu with your legs not quite as spread of dropping down to a deep lunge. Just slightly lowered maybe part way. Cross your wrists, turn your palms upwards and lift them gently to the height of your head as you raise yourself upwards while inhaling. There, turn your hands away from each other and form a large outwards circle with them and let them gently slide down again as you drop back downwards on the exhale.

Rolling Tai Ji

You perform this exercise in the horse stance. Put your weight on your left leg and lean your upper body to the right. The left hand is at hip level and points upwards, while the right hand is at shoulder level. Imagine that you are lifting a big ball. Now slide with this ball in the opposite direction. Change sides and shift your weight to your right leg.

As Mentioned, this is a simple verbal description so if it is not making sense, I am positive you can look these up on the internet to see a video. When I do these with the class, I find it helpful to stress the breathing to be timed with the movements of the action so that in a short time you can feel the energy moving with you on several of these. More advanced moves are also available that also serve to assist in moving energy as well as healing the body and since we do not speak about visualization with this, it allows the students to use their other senses in a common setting where sometimes you will feel the energy move from one hand to another or when we do 'push the ball' or 'firing the arrow' they will feel an effect from the person opposite of them.

One last thing for energy movement, before we move on to the next step. This chapter has been pretty reticent to take on the traditional approach of visualization for energy movement, as I want to impart a totally different approach, but if you have a partner that you work closely with, one final fun exercise to play with I will offer up. While this also removes visualization as a key factor, it is also a nice challenge for your opened hand chakras and your ability to 'feel' the energy you are moving/sensing.

Stand about two feet apart and open your hand chakras so you can feel that energy pulse you have become familiar with. One partner closes their eyes while you both hold your palms up facing each other, palms maybe an inch or so apart. The person who has their eyes open, 'pushes' energy into the palm of the other whose eyes are closed so that they try to 'feel' that energy. When they say they can feel it, the person with open eyes will slowly move their hand up, down, left, or right as they wish.

The person whose eyes are closed, needs to pay attention to the energy flow. You can 'sense' it is getting lighter on one section of your hand, so you know to move your hand towards the energy. Do this with each hand and maybe later with both at the same time and the results can be both fun and entertaining, but most importantly, it teaches you to focus your other senses on the energy, while simultaneously teaching you control of it at the same time.

CHAPTER THIRTEEN
SACRED SPACE

Wicca is often thought of as a loosely structured, or completely unstructured spiritual tradition, and for many people who were raised in more formal organized religions, this is definitely part of the draw. Nonetheless, there is a core feature of Wicca that serves to bring people together around a collective focus: Wiccan rituals-creation of sacred space.

Whether the occasion is a Sabbat, an Esbat, or a milestone such as a handfasting (wedding), an initiation, or an end-of-life ceremony, covens, and circle members will gather to worship together, honor the Goddess and God, and celebrate the wonders to be found in the ongoing cycles of life. While most Wiccan rituals are held in private, some covens will occasionally hold theirs in public, so that all who wish to observe can come and learn more about paganism. Many Wiccan circles do the same and may even invite the public to participate. Of course, solo rituals are no less significant, and solitary Wiccans know that as they worship at each point along the Wheel of the Year, they are adding their personal light and power to the collective magical energy on these special occasions.

Wiccan Ritual Basics

Beautiful, mysterious, elegant, and comforting, Wiccan rituals can take many different forms, with no two events being exactly alike. Some may be highly structured and elaborate. This is often the case with coven rituals, though since most covens keep the details of their rituals secret, known only to initiated members, it's difficult to describe them with much accuracy. Other rituals, particularly those practiced by solitary and eclectic Wiccans, may be fairly simple by comparison, and may even be made up on the spot.

The content of any given Wiccan ritual will depend on the occasion. For example, Esbats, or Full Moon celebrations, are focused solely on the Goddess, while Sabbats honor the co-creative relationship between the Goddess and the God. Despite all the possible variations, however, there are a few basic elements that tend to be included in what we might call a "typical" ritual. There are certain basic elements that should be incorporated in each ritual. They are as follows: Intent, Purification, Grounding, Creation of Sacred Space, Invoke/Evoke, Working, Cakes and Ale/Wine, Closing of the Sacred Space.

I always recommend that the initial step is to Set up the altar for the occasion. Just like we discussed the alter as a tool in chapter eleven, some will have one permanently set up, but may need to update the cloth, flowers, or whatnot for the specific ritual being performed that night…or set up their personal 'temporary' alter. In either case, it will likely be decorated differently depending on the occasion, such as bringing in fall foliage for the Autumn Equinox or Samhain. The altar is arranged with the various Wiccan tools, symbols, and offerings, laid out according to any one of a number of traditions. This helps set the mood you want for the ritual.

First, the Intent of the occasion is stated by all listening to the words for that nights activities—whether it's to celebrate a Sabbat or an Esbat, or perhaps to petition the God and Goddess on behalf of someone who needs healing or some other kind of assistance. (Magical spell work can indeed be the focus of a ritual, though many Wiccans will do this separately from Sabbat celebrations, so as to keep the focus on the Goddess and God during Sabbats.) This is typically an informal review of what is to take place along with expectations for the results.

After the intent is stated, the main body of the ritual may consist of various activities. The focal point may be the performance of a ritual drama—such as reenacting scenes from ancient myths or poems—or other liturgical material, depending on the tradition of Wicca the group is following. Solitary Wiccans might also read from ancient mystical texts or compose their own poetry for the occasion. Chanting, singing, dancing and/or other ritual gestures may be part of the proceedings, as might simply reflecting informally on the blessings of the season. Prayers might be offered, whether they are personal or on the behalf of others. In fact, it's common in some traditions to use ritual space to intend for the benefit of an entire community, or even all of humanity. If working in a coven, the actual parts of the ritual may be handed out to individuals to perform that portion of the rite. Remember, this is a participatory sport, so no sitting on the sidelines!

Next is the grounding. This brings all of the group down to a level where the work can begin and allows each to focus. You may recall some of the grounding techniques from Chapter Eight. Then of course is centering and if in a group, you should start to feel the energy of the others in the group, so you can work as a well-tuned machine at the time of the working. Sometimes this is as a small push of energy to the left if you're all holding hands or maybe a quick 'pass it on' kiss, but the main idea is to know how everyone is a single part of a greater group working towards a specific target.

Now, there is a purification, done for both the celebrant(s) and the place where the ritual is held. This can happen in the form of a ritual bath, and/or a smudging ceremony to remove any unwanted energies from the ritual space, whether it's an outdoor area or inside the home. Smudging involves the burning of sacred herbs, such as sage, rosemary, and/or lavender. Many times, if the group is cleansing or blessing the Elements, this will be incorporated into this action by first blessing the elements and then using them to cense and asperge the area and then the participants. Some groups will even use ritual scourging as part of the purification process.

Next comes the casting of the circle, an act that creates a boundary between the sacred space and the ordinary, mundane world. The altar is typically at the center or Northern most point of the circle, with plenty of room for all involved to work freely within the circle, with no accidental stepping outside of the energetic boundary. The circle may be marked with sea salt, a long cord, several stones, herbs, or candles. Some, when they work indoors, actually state that the circle boundaries are the walls of the room they are in.

There are many methods for circle-casting, some as simple as walking the circle with the wand or athame while chanting a script to focus the energy. I like to point out once again that this is a participatory sport, so, you should be lending your energy to the creation of the sacred space if you are not the one casting. IF you are the one casting, try to focus your coven mates energy through you into the tool used to strengthen the creation of your shield or bubble. You contribute by either performing these acts or contributing your energy to assist in making it happen. Depending on what tradition you follow, who you are taught by, or any other myriad of things, you may envision or feel the circle as a glowing, luminous wall, a brightly glowing line on the ground or some semitransparent dome surrounding you.

It's important at this time to note that while the visualization is simply a line or small wall, this is not just a wall you are creating around the area you are working, but more like an elliptical ball or egg-shaped sphere. It goes under you, around you and over you. It may glow with a purplish white light, or as some see it a hazed blur. The visualization is not what's important, but that you can feel the actual circle being raised and maybe the 'gooseflesh' that is raised if you are that inclined.

Once the circle is cast, the invocations begin. It may be a good time to differentiate between Invoke and Evoke: Invoke means to call upon, while Evoke is to call forth. Put in a different manner, to Invoke a deity is to call upon it and ask it to join you during ritual a working. Sometimes this involves simply asking ("Hail, Odin, we ask you to join us in the circle tonight!") or by making an offering ("Great Brigid, we offer you this bread as a gift of thanks!") in hopes that the deity will turn up in ritual.

Evoking, on the other hand, is a form of voluntary possession. When you Evoke a deity, you're not asking it to come hang out, you're inviting it into yourself, and that god or goddess will manifest, or come forth, through a human host. This is a very advanced aspect, that I would never perform alone or with inexperienced practitioners!

The order here can vary, but typically the four Elemental Guardians of the base Elements: Earth, Air, Fire, and Water are invited to join the ritual, as these are the raw materials that make up all of existence. (In many traditions, a fifth Element—Akasha, or Spirit—is also called in.) In many traditions, this step is known as Calling the Quarters, or the four directions (North, East, South, and West) are then addressed, either instead of or in addition to the Elements.

A slight differentiation to make is that at the beginning, you blessed or purified the Elements on your alter to help you purify the sacred space you are about to create. So, now you are calling upon the next level up (on the chain of command so to speak) with the quarters. These may be the Elemental itself (such as for Air, Fire, Water and Earth) or you may be requesting that the Guardian of said element come forward to watch over your rite. This can take the form of an elemental, and angel or even a normal person. What's important here is that you realize you are speaking to the next level up in the chain of command so a little discretion or politeness will go a long way.

Let me pause for a moment and speak on salutes to the quarters. Some people flip a quick salute, like a fencer does with their weapon, at the end of the summoning of the Elemental Guardian, some do nothing, and others draw fanciful pentagrams based on the element. I admit that this is what we teach so let me show you the way it is done.

Since there are Invoking and Banishing versions for each Element, let's go through how to draw that first.

```
        1-Spirit.

5-Air.                    2-Water.


4-Earth.        3-Fire.
```

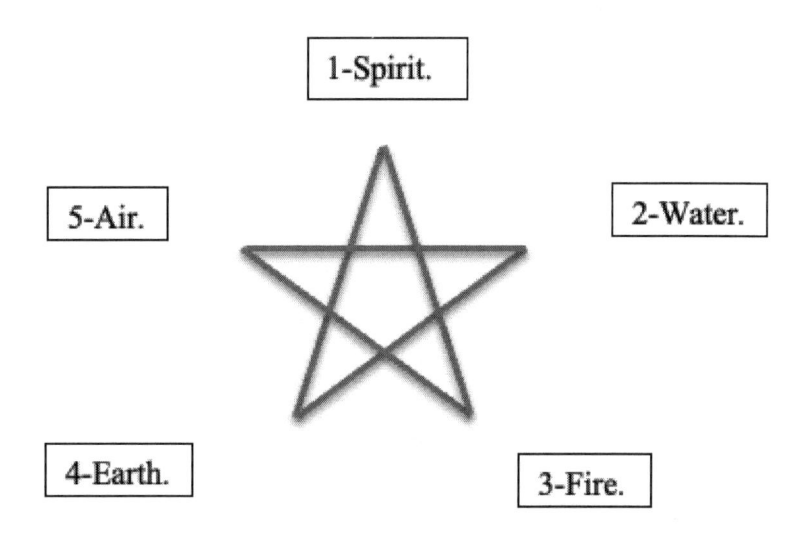

Below are the directions for Invoking and banishing each elemental pentagram:

Earth Invoking – 1, 4, 2, 5, 3, 1
Earth Banishing – 4, 1, 3, 4, 2, 4

Air Invoking – 2, 5, 3, 1, 4, 2
Air Banishing – 5, 2, 4, 1, 3, 5

Fire Invoking – 1, 3, 5, 2, 4, 1
Fire Banishing – 3, 1, 4, 2, 5, 3
Water Invoking – 5, 2, 4, 1, 3, 5
Water Banishing – 2, 5, 3, 1, 4, 2

Now, to be honest, recalling all of that is very confusing, can disrupt the energy if done improperly, or at a minimum, make the smooth transition of energy flag. Many practitioners, (yes including me as this is what I was taught), will only use the Earth

Pentagram for all elements, as they all come from the Goddess who is our Earth Mother. On the flip side, Counter Argument, I know several hard-core traditionalists who have memorized them all and use them all as they feel it is appropriate to use the proper pentagram for the proper Element and that it makes a profound difference on the level of consecration or attention from said Guardian.

Then the God and Goddess are Invoked/Evoked, for this is a worship religion after all. (Some groups may only call upon the one God or Goddess as they see fit or due to tradition). Since you are calling these deities to come visit your home away from home, it is always good manners to treat them with the utmost respect, just like you would a trusted and loved relative. My old school may be showing when I say that the Divine you have asked to join you is now a guest in your Sacred Space, so your best manners and good etiquette should be on display for them.

Show them you are happy for their presence (a simple Hello or Welcome is all that's needed). Give them the first sip of your wine and the first taste of your cakes, thank them for joining you, and when they leave, let them know you were happy they showed up! (again, a simple thank you may be all you need or go all the way and thank them for showing up to assist in your rite or the wisdom they imparted).

Once these steps have taken place, the heart of the ritual begins with this maybe being the working (Spell craft) or the drama enacted, poems chanted or whatever activity is deemed appropriate for that Sabbat or Esbat. This will, of course, be by your own experience, teachings, and your own predilections as the choices here are infinite and varied as the number of traditions out there today.

In many traditions, a ceremony known as "cakes and ale" (or "cakes and wine") is an important part of Wiccan rituals. Food and drink are offered and symbolically shared with the God and Goddess, typically at the end of the body of the ritual (Although some traditions begin with it, and again, I feel the Divine should get the first taste of each symbolically offered by placing it into the libation dish/cup). This ceremony connects the spiritual plane with the Earth plane and helps to ground and center the participants after the expenditure of energy to perform the spell craft. This is also a symbolic representation of the 'Great Rite' according to many initiatory traditions. It shows the athame entering the cup, and you may recall we talked about how the athame is male or God representation to the cups female or Goddess representation, so the two conjoined in such a manner is a symbolistic magic all its own.

When it's time to end the ritual, the Elements and the Goddess and God are formally thanked and released, the quarter guardians are thanked as well, and the circle is closed in a similar manner as to when the sacred space was erected. Below is just a basic template that a Wiccan ritual may typically follow. If you join an established coven or circle, the group will most likely have its own version of what's been described above, with many possible variations. If you're a solitary practitioner, you can research a specific tradition to follow, or you can create your own unique Wiccan rituals.

Our Outer Court has specific scripts that we use and the participants are expected to learn them as part of the process. Once initiated, we have a specific Inner Court script that has been handed down throughout the line we are a part of. Below is a simple version of that Outer Court script for your use if you like.

You may want to incorporate your own little flairs or remove items you do not think required. I would advise you to refrain from removing too much, as it can change the energy flows so you may not be as protected as you may need to be during some ritual.

ADDITIONAL RITUAL SCRIPT

You can use this as a basic Full Moon script or even for a Sabbat if you choose (speaking in **bold** font) You don't have to use this verbatim. You can update it to fit your style, circumstances, the ritual desire, or Sabbat celebration. :

> **Preface:** Light all your candles, quarters, alter, etc. and start the charcoal in the censor or cauldron if you use one.
>
> - Perform a grounding with all people. (see the example in chapter eight)
> - Tap the wand on the alter three times. Ring your bell three times.
> - Insert your athame into the elements for consecration, raise each one after performing the consecration: (add incense as needed)
>
> **WATER: "I exorcise thee oh creature of water casting out all darkness and uncleanliness in the names of our Lord and Lady."**
>
> **EARTH: "Blessing be upon you creature of Earth, casting out all darkness and illusion, calling forth good to aid us in our work for the Lord and Lady."**

AIR: "I exorcise thee, creature of air, casting out all weakness and vice, calling forth strength and virtue in the names of our Lord and Lady."

FIRE: "Blessings upon thee, creature of fire, casting out shadow and fear, bringing forth light and courage in the names of our Lord and Lady."

Asperge the circle and then the participants. Incense the circle and then the participants. Perhaps you perform a simple chant while this is taking place. Create the sacred space by tracing with either your wand, Athame or sword and say: **"I conjure and create thee Oh Circle of Power, a boundary between the worlds that protects against all evil powers and spirits, so that all within shall be duly protected and all powers shall be contained in the names of our Lord and Lady."**

"So Mote it be!" *Response from all:* **"So Mote it be!"**

Next perform the summoning of the elemental guardians by facing each cardinal point (Face East, South, West then North with a final bow to the east to complete the circle once again) holding athame forward and intone the following: **"Guardians of the watchtowers of the ____, rulers of ____, I do summon stir and call you up to witness our rites and guard this circle."**

Invocation to the Sun and Moon: **"Lady, we call upon you to join us in your glory and hear our prayers as we worship at your feet."**

"Lord, grant us thy protection when you join us and sing with us in celebration as we worship at your feet."

Working:
Perform whatever worship or work is needed.

Cakes and Ale:
High Priest holds athame into the cup of ale that is held by High Priestess and intones:

"As the athame is to the God, so the cup is to the Goddess, And so conjoined they become one in truth."

This drink is now shared among the participants with offerings to the Goddess and God added to a libation cup. In my opinion, the way I was taught, that you should offer the libation to the God and Goddess prior to your own partaking in an effort to show respect and reverence. Pass to each person clockwise.

The High Priest then blesses the cakes with their wand or athame while the plate is held by the High Priestess and intones: **"Oh, Queen most secret, bless this food to our bodies that it may bestow health, wealth, joy, and peace, and that love which is perfect happiness."**

Once again, pass the items clockwise so all can partake with the God and Goddess served first. When all have been served and the discussion turns to more mundane items, the ritual is formally ended by the High Priestess who takes up her athame and says: **"Witches all, our mysteries ended, may we thank the mighty ones who have graced us with their presence, therefore comes the charge to lock away all our secrets within your hearts, and may the Gods preserve the craft!"**

Group response: **"May the Gods preserve the craft!"**

Now dismiss the elemental guardians by facing each cardinal point with raised athame and intone to each direction (East, South, West and North with a bow back to the East): **"Guardians** of the watchtowers of the _____, Rulers of _____, We thank you for attending our rites and guarding our circle, we wish you hale and farewell."

Group responds with: **"Hail and farewell."** The circle is lifted by the High Priestess with her athame while intoning: **"Oh, circle of power, that has been created as a boundary of protection against all evil powers and spirits, that has duly protected and guarded all within, shall you now dissolve and return to the earth from whence you came."**

"The circle is now open; the Goddess blesses her children."

"So Mote it be!"

Response from all: **"So Mote it be"**

Now, let's talk about the whys of what was done above.

Preface: Light all your candles, quarters, alter, etc. and start the charcoal in the censor or cauldron if you use one.

This is done to prepare not only your space, but to prepare you and have you start to think about your intent for what lays ahead.

Perform a grounding with all people.

Grounding and centering with a group awareness is critical to your ability to focus energy, have everyone on the same page, and to start to change your consciousness from the mundane to the spiritual.

Tap the wand on the alter three times. Ring your bell three times.

Tapping the wand (which is a male aspect) is like knocking on the door of the Gods home to get his attention, just like the Bell is a female aspect, it also gets the attention of the Goddess. I also like to believe it signals a clear 'starters gun' to the ritual.

Insert your athame into the elements for consecration, raise each one after performing the consecration.

Here is where you are consecrating the elements so you can use purified items for the creation of your sacred space. You can leave the salt, water, etc. behind as consecration does not decay. You do this for cleansing the space, yourselves, and also to insure that you now have removed any negativity that may have attached to them if you leave them out each day. As some will say, "once consecrated, always consecrated."

I think it never hurts to continually consecrate the same salt, water, etc., as it only builds upon itself to drive home the divine in it. Also, using this item right away is always a good idea, so presenting it to the gods in supplication, is to show your work, but then using the mixtures of Water and Earth, Fire and Air to purify and bless your space and individuals accomplishes this!

Asperge the circle and then the participants. Incense the circle and then the participants.

First you must wash the space to purify it, then you perfume the space to make it pleasant. In my earlier training I was told that you walk the circle three times with these two being the first and always and in this order. You would not perfume yourself and then take a bath when getting ready, so you are washing away impurities, cleansing the area and then the people. Then while you asperge, you are 'perfuming' the circle, so it is attractive to the God and Goddess just as you become from the same activities.

Create the sacred space by tracing with either your wand, Athame or sword.

Here we are creating the third circumference of our sacred space, remember the sacredness of three! You are erecting that boundary between worlds, between time and space, to shield you from wickedness and evil while you work the craft or worship the Lord and Lady. This is where you are creating that threshold to protect you while you are in communication with the Divine.

Next, perform the summoning of the elemental guardians by facing each cardinal point (Face East, South, West then North with a final bow to the east to complete the circle once again) holding athame forward and intone the following:

You call upon them to witness your rites and assist in your communication to either the Elementals or the Divine. Sometimes it may be to much for a person to speak to the Divine or the Elementals as they are on a completely different level than us. Think of it as you are calling upon an Angel of God to speak on your behalf, much like you would a lawyer to speak to a judge so as to protect you or warn you of any untoward happenstances.

Invocation to the Sun and Moon:

You call upon the God and Goddess to join you for worship, blessings, to ask for assistance or guidance just as you would in any other religion after all!

Working: Perform whatever worship or work is needed.

Cakes and Ale:

This serves several functions. First you are making an offering or sacrifice to the Gods by placing the drink and food into the libation. I always try to stress that you provide to them first and then yourself as they are the preeminent reason for your being in this religion after all. Second, it is a time to recoup some of the energies you have expended while summoning the Divine and/or performing your ritual or spell work. Lastly it is a great opportunity to discuss the ritual (sort of a postmortem if you will) so you can recognize that John slipped up at this while Joan slipped up on that so you can perform better next time. It's important here to realize that you are discussing the mechanics of the ritual and not so much the working as this may inhibit the working from 'going out and doing' while you hold on.

The ritual is formally ended by the High Priestess who starts the ending with her Statement

This is a formal delineation from 'cakes and wine' to closing the circle and preparing you onto your journey back to the mundane. It is also a note to make you once again aware of the fact that you are in Sacred Space, to guard against speaking about what happened in ritual and a hope that the Wicca persists.

Now dismiss the elemental guardians.

This now formally releases the guardians back to their realm so they can continue on with business. You may note that this process is an opposite order from the building, just as you take a path to get to a place, you normally reverse that path to get back. I do not recommend walking widdershins (counterclockwise) like starting in the West and going to South, etc. as that would be disruptive or bad manners as it were. Always reface the East and perform a final salute to close that circle, because if you just stopped after doing the Northern, it would leave a gap in that circular completeness we strived so strongly for at the beginning.

The circle is lifted by the High Priestess with her athame.

There are some who say you do not need this as by walking across the threshold you drop it anyways, but it just seems good manners to dismiss the circle after creating it. Remember that the creation moved you to a place between, so dropping it in a similar fashion also brings you back from between, to the here and now.

Lastly is the MM, MP, MMA (Merry Meet, Merry Part, Merry Meet Again) statement. I know so many who take this for granted as just a really nice loving closing statement but let's take a moment to really examine what this is saying. "Merry Meet," is a statement of coming together for fellowship as is told to us in the charge of the Goddess. She directs us to meet in some secret place and adore the spirits of the Goddess.

"Merry Part" is a signal that we must leave each other after the completion of this fellowship, but that we do so in Perfect Love and Trust as this truth has set us free. "Merry Meet Again" is the credo, if you will, to repeat our meetings. Again, the words from the charge state 'once a month' so this dictates repetition of our meetings.

CHAPTER FOURTEEN
DEDICATION AND INITIATION

Just like we did in the beginning with 'what is wicca, paganism and the craft,' let's take a look at the definitions of Initiation and Self-Dedication:

> **Initiation:** the action of admitting someone into a secret or obscure society or group, typically with a ritual.
>
> **Self-Dedication:** a feeling or promise of very strong support or commitment to something.

This has two very important items we should speak on that may be important information. First, is that an initiation is given from a group, and the dedication is performed for and by yourself. Second, most groups or covens will not initiate until after you have been through their wicca 101 or spent some period of time working with them, so since this entails a considerable commitment, I advise caution on just diving into any coven you can. Make sure you and THEY are a good fit as a group as in most covens, you will work very closely together.

Many newcomers to Wicca are curious about the process of

initiation. What exactly is involved? Do you have to be initiated before you can truly be a Wiccan? Answers to these questions can vary from person to person, but below you'll find my perspective on initiation and self-dedication.

Not everyone who wants to explore Wicca as a potential spiritual path will stick with it. Some people find themselves drawn to this religion for a while, but eventually realize that it's not for them. Others may discover Wicca as a starting point to a broader, less defined spiritual path that may have some similar beliefs and practices, but ultimately isn't Wiccan.

And then there are those who truly find themselves at home in this world, who will eventually decide that they want to dedicate themselves to following the Wiccan path as a way of life. For this last group, the question of initiation will inevitably present itself. But just what is initiation, and how do you go about setting it in motion? What is involved in the Wiccan initiation ceremony itself? The answers depend on whether you want to practice Wicca among others within a coven or forge a solo path of your own making.

They also depend on if you have worked with a group and decide to form a coven or are joining an existing coven that is focused on a specific tradition. If you are forming your own group, you get to decide what is what and who to work with, but if joining an initiatory tradition like Gardnerian, Alexandrian or Faerie, they already have set rituals for this as well as expectations on what you will be doing to advance. Dedication comes with no groups, no conditions besides the ones you set, and no 'levels' of experience. It is all about you and your promise to the Lord and Lady, personal, close, and free flowing one to the other.

Initiation into a mystery tradition like those above come with commitments to a group, specific ways of doing things, but most importantly to some, a lineage that traces back to a specific person…i. e. , like to Gerald Gardener in the Gardnerian tradition. You also get the background and support of an entire group that does things the same way (mostly) that you do and are ultimately taught to grow into the priesthood so you can start a coven of your own. Does one make you a 'better' Wiccan than the other? Does one gain more magical ability, learn more spells, get closer to the God and Goddess?

The answers to those are no, no, no and shocker, no! However, you may experience greater highs and lows in a group setting due to the way people working in a group (whether that is a lose group of friends or an actual mystery tradition coven) as you now have more humans in sacred space effecting the outcome. The thing to remember is that if you decide one way, you can always go the other, it just may take longer to achieve your goals than had you chosen that path in the beginning. If you are lucky, you fall into a group right out of the gate, (not all that common an occurrence) or you start a Wicca 101 course and bond immediately.

I should be very upfront and remind you that each coven is always different due to the people that make it up, not the tradition that it represents. So, you may find a group right away, but the normal thing that happens is you start to read books, you may attend a few public rituals, make a few likeminded friends along the way, and then decide you want to get into a coven that is mystery tradition like the above types I mentioned.

You still have to petition or work with them for a period of time…so many older groups still stick to the 'year and a day' axiom, but that can be a negotiated time based on fit, experience, or any number of things. It is up to the coven to decide, once you ask for initiation, to determine yes or no. There is no entitlement to initiation, no 'I think I am ready so you should initiate me' approach. You ask, they answer. However, it is also just as important to realize it is a two-way street!

You may work with this group for three months and think they are totally dysfunctional and request to leave on good terms, they may tell you no, for whatever reason…you're not a good fit, you don't drink alcohol and they do so it creates an imbalance, your energy is still not as focused…whatever the reason is, this is not a disparagement of you. This is important to understand! Them saying no is not all about you being bad in some way, it is about the fit between the existing coven group and you and how well it meshes.

It could very well be that they are just not accepting seekers at this time, or something else has come up internally in the coven. Never stop looking for that group if that is what you want. Sometimes that group is found while at a Pagan Ways retreat or festival, a flyer for a Wicca 101 is flown at the local bookstore, you know a guy. There may be many 'No's' before you get that 'yes', but the patience is worth it. Once you initiate, your life changes. I do not mean this as changes from a neophyte to a witch, but from one level of consciousness to another. The experience of being initiated will affect you heart and soul (I know it did me, and many of my initiates since have said the same thing) so that your life takes on a whole new meaning.

Just the experience of training your body to feel the ebb and flow of nature, the tides changing once again as the pull of the moon increases and wanes. These things alone will change you, but add in the sabbats, the magic of the initiation, and you will be affected. I am not trying to push initiation, so much as make you aware that it may affect you more than a dedication will as well as some of the differences between them. Let's now discuss some of the things that surround either a Self-Dedication or even the Initiation as both have their merits and pitfalls.

SELF-DEDICATION

A Wiccan Rite of Dedication is in lieu of an initiation because you really need the help of other people to experience that in its full impact. But you can undertake a solo ritual of dedication. You'll find them online, you'll find them in other traditions but they're very important for somebody, especially somebody who's working alone. It's an opportunity for you to make a commitment.

One of the first things that I was taught in the Wicca 101 course that I studied in, a long time ago, was that when you make a promise, when a witch makes a promise, it must be kept. So, a self-dedication ritual is a promise that you make to yourself. It's a promise to go in pursuit of your purpose. It's a promise to go in pursuit of the sacred that lies within you and to seek it in the world around you which is incredibly challenging given the culture and crazy world that we're now living in as a result of that culture.

Since it's a commitment that you make to yourself, nobody else is going to enforce it for you, so, it requires a certain amount of courage and self-discipline and devotion. Which is why it's called a Rite of Self Dedication. You are pledging yourself to your future and to the fullness of your Spiritual journey. I can assure you that when you embark on this path it's a future that's full of the richness of the sacred and divine magic.

For solitary Wiccans, the path to initiation and even the terminology associated with it is less than clear cut. Rather than *initiation*, the more widely recognized term for a solitary Witch's formal entrance into the Craft is *self-dedication*. A ritual of self-dedication may resemble aspects of a coven initiation to varying degrees, but because solitary Witches can design and perform this ritual in any way they like, it is a fundamentally different experience.

Self-dedication happens strictly on your own terms. The commitment you're declaring in such a ritual is really to your inner self, to any deities you may incorporate into your practice, and/or to the divinity of the Universe as you understand it. It's not a commitment to any other person, or an entrance into a group of fellow practitioners. And since this experience is strictly between you and the divine, you can call it whatever you like, self-dedication, self-initiation, married or something else entirely, if that's what makes the most sense to you.

Although this is a very different experience from that of a coven initiation, there are still important parallels on the journey to this milestone on your path. First, of course, is the work of really getting a feel for the Wicca—exploring possible avenues in terms of established traditions, getting a sense for what resonates with you and what doesn't, and continuing to read as much and as widely as you can. It's traditionally recommended to spend a year and a day studying the Wicca before undertaking your self-dedication, but you can certainly take longer if you like.

Once you feel ready to take steps toward dedication, you can start thinking about what this ritual will look like for you. If you'd like to take a structured approach to the process, you can find Wiccan books and online resources that will offer you a well-defined plan, from interactive classes to recommended book lists and more. If you're looking to follow a specific, established practice rather than building your own eclectic form, you can find some good contemporary models all over the internet or any occult bookshop.

You can find some of these in the recommended reading list I have as the next chapter. (There is certainly some good stuff on this subject in the Farrar, Buckland, and Cunningham books and Thorn Mooney does a superior job in her book speaking about searching for covens and in talking about initiation) Many of these classic books provide plenty of practical information, including detailed rituals for self-dedication that you can follow to the letter, if you wish.

If you're more eclectically inclined, you will probably want to borrow from more than one tradition as you develop your practice. But you can still set yourself a course of study to follow as you work your way toward the point where you feel ready for initiation. You can set up a syllabus of items similar to what is in this book or push it to specific items like Tarot Divination or the Norse pantheon, or maybe you want to study a specific tradition like Gardnerian so you could assign yourself specific goals to read these books, study that film review information from Gardnerian Facebook pages even.

The key is to give yourself a certain amount of reading per week, organize your studies around specific topics you have chosen as your syllabus, and/or read all the books written by a particular author before moving on to a new one. Then again, you may want to be more free-wheeling and non-methodical about your study, following your inner guide from moment to moment until you're thoroughly inspired to perform your self-dedication.

When it comes to the Wiccan dedication ritual itself if you haven't found one you want to follow in any of the sources you've consulted, then you will need to design your own. You may want to piece your process together from various sources, possibly including some details from your own inspiration. You may even invent one entirely from scratch and on the spot. Just know that the details are less important than your sincere desire to formalize your commitment to the Wiccan way of life. You can even ask the Goddess and God to help you choose your best approach through meditations, divinations, or dream journeys. The key is that you take that step of dedication and stick to it as part of your promise to work this path for a period of time. Maybe you choose to renew your dedication on a yearly basis or use it as a steppingstone to locate an active coven in your area. It's all up to you.

COVEN INITIATION

For most people, the word *initiation* brings to mind a secret ceremony in which a person is admitted into a specific Organization like some daunting college fraternity movie with all the weird hype and crazy shenanigans. Nothing could be further from the truth. An initiation is a life changing achievement like a Wedding, a Bar-mitzvah or Quinceanera. If your aim is to join a traditional coven, then this is an apt description.

In Wicca, the classic sense of initiation involves the passing down of specific traditions from one Witch to another. For any lineage system, like Alexandrian, Gardnerian etc. would-be members of a coven will study under the mentorship of the initiated, experienced members until they are knowledgeable and practiced enough to participate in coven rituals, and, most importantly, to commit themselves to spiritual fellowship with the group. In keeping with the traditions of secrecy regarding some traditions, the vast majority of covens do not share the details of their initiation rituals with outsiders. However, there are some general characteristics that many coven processes have in common. I should say that the initiation is indeed a *process*, a series of steps leading up to an experience of spiritual transformation that involves, but is not limited to, the moment of the rite itself. Again, while this varies between traditions, let's review what you can expect.

First, the would-be initiate meets and spends time with the coven members, learning basic information about the coven's history and the tradition(s) they follow, and generally getting a sense for whether or not this particular group is a good fit. This is a crucial undertaking, for both the individual and the coven. A coven needs its members to be wholly committed to participating in rituals and contributing their energy on a consistent basis.

You often hear about studying for a 'year and a day' and while it takes us about that long to go through this book which is based on our Wicca 101 course, it may be longer or shorter for some people or courses. The idea is to expose you to the basics of the religion and the Craft, so you have a background to base your decision of Dedication vs Initiation on. The other part of this course and that time working together is to determine how well each person meshes with the others.

If you do find a good fit and decide to begin the initiation process, you will then enter a period of study and mentorship with one or more experienced members of the coven. During this time, you'll be immersing yourself in the beliefs and practices followed by the coven, and depending on the coven's philosophies, possibly engaging in your own explorations of the Wicca as well. Once you're initiated, you will be responsible for keeping your commitments to the coven—to show up for rituals and other meetings, to honor vows of secrecy, and to be part of the support system that coven membership offers.

Initiation into a coven is not something to be taken lightly. You are entering into very strong emotional and spiritual bonds with the individuals in this group, so you need to be truly compatible with them. In fact, some Witches, as I mentioned above, have likened initiation to marriage, or being adopted into a family, and many people find that they are closer to their fellow coven-mates than they are to their own family.

Besides the time spent working with the coven group prior to the initiation, you can expect that day to be a gauntlet of emotions, a life changing experience that strips you down to the bare and rebuilds you up again, in the before said, transformative experience, but at the end you are typically oathbound to that group, so I recommend it be done on a Friday or Saturday, so you have time to recover mentally and sometimes physically. Initiations are often performed in tier or level format so you may get your first degree which typically means you are learning, then a second which shows you have gained that knowledge, and finally a third which shows you as a leader or Priest/Priestess. The time between degrees may vary greatly from person to person or group to group but is typically that same year and a day referenced for your time learning the Wicca initially.

Don't ever join a coven just because you want to belong to a group of Witches, or you are likely to regret your choice. Indeed, it's definitely better to practice on your own than to become bound to a situation that is anything less than joyful, caring, and fulfilling.

THE JOURNEY INTO THE LABYRINTH

Initiation/self-dedication is a personal decision that no one can make for you. Unless you are seeking official membership in a traditional mystery coven, it's actually an entirely optional experience. But whether or not you seek initiation, know that a single ritual is not going to suddenly catapult you into a full-blown magical existence, or guarantee that you'll stay on this particular path forever. There are Witches who have practiced all their lives without undergoing initiation, and plenty of initiated ones who lost interest in Wicca down the road. Throughout your life, it will be up to you to continue choosing the path, in your own way and at your own pace.

Some traditions will speak about the duality of sexes being important, so opposite sexes initiate the other into the Wicca, while some have same sex initiations or some combination of both. I am sure that whatever path into the Wicca you chose, it will be the right one for you. Once you start down this path, it is typically a lifelong commitment, but again, some find it not to be the answer they were looking for and take another turn at some other religion.

All of this reflects the multitude of ways you can touch the divine in yourself or even in the Lord and Lady. Go forth my friends and fellow Witches and do great magics, teach others of the Wicca, and fellowship as you can with others as it is a great opportunity to see things from a different point of view, learn new Craft, skills or get a connection to a group near you that just may be the one thing missing from your spiritual growth.

Just to retouch on some things mentioned throughout the book, you are doing your own research via the internet, local bookstores, other people, or however you do it, that process is not a 15-minute Google search and done. Take that time to really review what it says about the coven or tradition you are interested in. Meet with them in a public place over coffee or ice cream and ask pertinent questions about themselves, the wicca, the tradition, their experience, etcetera, as they will certainly, ask these same questions of you! Think of these meetings as extended job interviews so come prepared, listen before responding, take notes if needed, so you can refer back to them later and have questions set up just for them.

Good luck in your endeavors and welcome to the spiral dance my friend! Bright Blessings of the God and Goddess be with you always!

Chapter Fifteen
Recommended Reading List

A Witch's Bible – Janet and Stewart Farrar
   This is a wonderful, if dated book on early BTW (British Traditional Wicca) tradition by two very well-spoken authors for their time and it has nice photos, and detailed information on the growth of Wicca from the early 1950s.

Wicca: A guide to Solitary Practitioner – Scott Cunningham
   Scott does a nice paced easy read with some simple and easy to follow instructions that help many get started.

Modern Guide to Witchcraft – Skye Alexander
   She will carefully guide you through many different spells, incantations, and ritual to help personalize them all.

Drawing Down the Moon – Margot Adler
   This is a wonderful accounting of that activity done by the HPS of a coven with trancework allowing the Goddess to speak with her lips.

Spiral Dance – Starhawk

This is the classic book on Wiccan and Spiritual feminization with the Goddess movement. She writes with an easy, fluid manner that allows for quick comprehension.

Witchcraft Today – Gerald B. Gardener

Considering that this was written in the mid-1950s, this book has nice thoughts on the history and practices as seen through the eyes of the father of Wicca.

Witchcraft for Tomorrow – Doreen Valiente

Doreen takes Gerald's book a step farther, incorporating many other occult techniques and cultures that updates to many ideals of today.

Traditional Wicca – Thorn Mooney

This is an incredible read as Thorn takes on some truly strong opinions on today's Wicca and says them in such a way that they remove the hard-core traditionalist approach and explain them in a simple logical manner.

Real Magic – Isaac Bonewits

In an almost scholarly manner, this book portrays magic as a logical progression from point "A" to point "B" that will have you saying 'Hmmm' while rubbing your chin and actually thinking about what he just told you!

The Mystical Qabalah – Dion Fortune

What I like about this is that it easily opens up and demystifies an almost 'high church/ceremonial magic' type of thinking that I make it a point to review it during our wicca 101 course as part of our ritual and tradition work.